GW00802036

Other Titles by this Author

On the Other Hand: The Little Anthology of Big questions

Louder than a Whisper: Clearer than a Bell

Stepping Out of Time

Umbra, Penumbra & Me (a compilation)

The Doubt Factor

Children's Picture Books

The Frightened Little Flower Bud   Ages 4-99

Hat   Ages 6-99

Walk straight ahead
Listen to no-one
Trust not in the walls or doorways
For they will mislead
And close behind you
As you walk through
The forest, not knowing
Where you've come from
Or where you're going …
If anywhere at all.

JUST AROUND THE BEND

Renée Paule

RPG Publishing

Just Around The Bend: Más o Menos

By Renée Paule

Edited by G R Hewitt

Published in France by RPG Publishing 2014

Cover design and artwork by Renée Paule

Written in British English

ISBN: 978-2-9546811-4-6

Thank You

Godfrey for believing in me
and for all your help and support.

~~~!

Aleena for so much inspiration

Mike

Anne

'little red ball'

Hazel

No jargon!

Humanity
Each and every one of us as a 'whole'.

One
All that is, was or ever will be.

Ignorant
To ignore.

Intelligence
Independent and radical thinking.

Society
The world we've created for ourselves to live in,
with all its complex mechanisms.

Belief
A personal preference.

Hope
Waiting for a future event that may never arrive.

Fear
Dreading a future event.

Spiritual
Thinking outside the box and searching inside
ourselves for higher meaning.

For your convenience there are blank pages
for notes at the back of this book.

Table of Contents

Preface

Remove yourself from the loop of self-destruction.

If you haven't read *On The Other Hand* you'll be unaware that I've been married six times (four officially). You might be asking yourself why I didn't learn the first time, or even the second or third. Some of you might want to know what went wrong, who was at fault and how things panned out. However, feasting on the bones of my past serves no good purpose and isn't the point of this book. Realising this was paramount to the decision I made not to publish my autobiography. I've looked closely at the repetitive patterns of my life and taken full responsibility for them, refusing to continue laying the blame elsewhere; I'm much happier now.

We can break the cycle of self-imprisonment, enforced only by the walls we constructed ourselves; quite often they're made of faux materials as once the mind gets hold of an idea it decorates it to its own particular style. I can assure you that although I've torn many walls down, I'm not more fortunate than you (far from it) neither am I stronger or luckier - I just made a decision not to live behind them anymore. The strength of these walls is proportional to the strength of our agreement to live our lives behind them. One of the toughest walls for me to remove was the one that prevented me from writing. Writing was an itch I just had to scratch and the greatest difficulty I faced was overcoming the belief that I couldn't reach the spot. Another itch told me I couldn't change and that I wasn't strong enough. I now recognise these as walls put up by my fierce resistance to responsibility and the negative influences of people around me, who I allowed to tell me I wasn't good enough.

The ordeals that tormented me in my youth became the weapons used in a war against the world. Imagine living in a world where we no longer believe that war can lead to peace. War can't lead to peace any more than ignorance can lead to knowledge. War leads to premature death, pain, suffering, hatred, fear and more separation. The hardest thing to understand in my childhood was why there are such cruelties in the world; I couldn't see why any one person would want to hurt or harm another. I had a feeling of helplessness inside me and felt powerless to change my life without outside help. This was mostly because I was always asking 'why' and remained focused on my own misery. We can always call for help but there's really no point, unless we're prepared to work in line with that call.

My war continued until I was ready and willing to bring an end to it - until I was willing to let go of fear. Torment only occurs inside us; it occurs because we hold on tightly to the very things we'd be better off letting go of. These things are created by the mind and it's maddened when we want to let go of them. The tools I utilised to find my way out of misery were tenacity, a willingness to let go of all attachment and a deep-seated knowledge that there's more to me than a human body.

All these removed me from what I was brought up to believe was a place of safety.

I explained in *On The Other Hand* why questioning is important and I asked something like four hundred and forty questions in it. I've asked myself many more since and I'm still asking them. Questioning brings about unlearning and therefore freedom from what has held us in our prison of conditioned beliefs. I've received several messages saying that the questions 'just kept on coming'. Yes they do and that's why I gave the book a subtitle; The Little Anthology of Big Questions. When I told a friend of mine I'd started writing another book, she asked me if it would have the answers in it. It won't, but if it did they wouldn't help anyone but me; they'd be my answers which aren't the same as yours and when I get an answer, I question it. We've had all our questions answered (or ignored) from the moment we could ask them, by the media, our parents, and teachers; society has been holding our hand, steering Humanity in the direction it wants it to go in. The answers have built up what we believe we know about the world and challenging those beliefs can be tough because they're deep-seated and driven by fear. Rather than being about finding more confusing answers, the questions are about challenging what we've come to accept as true. When challenging the truths we think we know, it's not necessary to replace them with others.

A lot has changed for me and many mornings I've woken up and wondered where I am, even though I'm still here. Most mornings my world feels like a different place to the one I went to sleep in the night before -

each day feels fresh and new. You're more than welcome to join me on my journey through this book. I feel like the waters are still flowing and I've not and don't expect to come to a halt. Paradoxically, I'm not going anywhere at all. It's not easy to challenge our world and it's certainly not easy to grasp some of these concepts, but it's worthwhile and doable. It's difficult because the majority of the world is racing in one direction and you and I - as you're reading this - have decided to go in another. I don't trust any information now other than what I've thought out and realised for myself. I haven't found answers, neither do I look for any, but I've found something that makes me feel driven and I know it's the only place worth driving to.

Introduction

*We got ourselves into this mess -
only we can get ourselves out of it.*

For those of you who've read my first book *On The Other Hand*, you'll be pleased to hear that there are fewer questions in this book. The reason being that once we start asking questions and observe our mind operating we realise how much control it has over our lives - it quietens. I've also decided to dispense with the need for a bibliography or quotes to support the things I write. With hindsight, I probably felt the need to back up some of my thoughts, but this is no longer the case; I prefer to speak in my own words, rather than the words of others. Anyone can see the things I've written - they're no secret. This is my voice and I'm reluctant to use any other now; my first chapter 'A Bit of a Rant' covers the subject of quotes a little more.

By observing our thought processes we tune in to a higher vibration - it's inevitable. At first we find it hard to let go of the familiar, because we've so much noise going on in our heads that we can't keep up with the pace. It's rather like listening to or watching two films simultaneously in fast forward - our two conflicting voices.

Before going any further I'd like to make it perfectly clear, for the fluidity of this book, that I use the pronoun we a great deal. This is how I see us; we are One. Yes, it's not always 100% appropriate to use the proverbial we but I don't intend to continually stop my train of thoughts to explain this. If you feel this 'we' doesn't apply to you then please feel free not to apply it - for the purposes of this book its meaning is general.

When we're on a journey of self-discovery the river flows so fast that it's hard to keep up with. We often have to slow down a bit and take stock while we catch our breath. Consequently, we miss much in the Now. Imagine being carried away by a fast-flowing river - you won't be able to see everything going on around you whilst trying to avoid going over the waterfall you're approaching. In the same way we can't see around the bend, or behind a curtain or door, but there comes a point when they no longer present obstacles because we're not afraid any more. As explained in *On The Other Hand* there's only the Here and Now; clearly the title of this book is a physical metaphor for somewhere metaphysically, far closer to home. We look to physical solutions for metaphysical puzzles; whatever we do physically won't provide a permanent solution.

For our woes we look to tranquillisers, anti-depressants, sleeping pills, alcohol, chocolate, mind-altering drugs, entertainments, things, someone-to-lean-on and psychotherapy, but we never seem to get well. We need to find solutions to our own problems or our healing won't be permanent. We can't change the hearts of others, not ever, so it really is a waste of time trying. If you doubt this then think about whether or not anyone can change you. Doctors are necessary for many illnesses and injuries but there are many other ailments that we can help ourselves with, such as depression or anxiety. One of the issues that would benefit Humanity to examine is why there's so much disease in the world, rather than how can we cure it? There are no medicines that can cure sadness, frustration, despair, loneliness or a broken spirit. We have to face these for ourselves in order to raise our level of consciousness. We can only do it Now by understanding the mind and how it controls us. We've become so used to conflicts and helplessness that challenging them is not something we're very good at. However, like falling off a bike while learning to ride it, we can get back on it again and ride off in any direction we choose. There's nothing keeping us down other than the thought that we can't, or don't want to, get up again.

Think about what self-help is. It's about helping ourselves without relying on assistance from any authority other than our own. We read and rave about new self-help books as we may the latest diet. These diets may help us to lose a few pounds and we feel better for it, but when we come off them again we regain the weight and often, more. When this happens we also suffer with disappointment in ourselves, lower self-esteem and higher levels of self-hatred. Any positive effects we feel are temporary and that can't be worth striving for; there has to be a permanent change of lifestyle in order to feel the positive benefits - it's an ongoing process.

There are those who experience an instant conversion from unconsciousness to Consciousness, but they're few and far between and the majority of us take a far longer road to Damascus. Many of us can be discouraged by 'epiphany' stories, particularly when we're told they're so rare; I was one of them. This book is for those of us who take longer to realise what we already know on one level and to keep you company on your 'journey'. Don't give up. It must happen if you want it to. We're never alone and never have been.

The author of a self-help book, more often than not, tells us how they found their way and this is not necessarily the right way for us, which is why the effects don't last. It's difficult enough to find out who we really are and even more difficult to walk in someone else's footsteps. For many years I looked outside for help and the more I tried to find it there, the more frustrated I became with the world and the more I withdrew into my shell. It wasn't until I finally understood that I already have all the power I'd ever need, right here and Now, that I took responsibility for myself. The most essential ingredient in that change is the will to put an end to our own pain and suffering instead of lackadaisically hoping someone else will change it all for us. When we're willing to raise our level of consciousness, we're helping ourselves, but as long as our focus and awareness are on our inability to do it, or we're waiting for someone else to administer a magic formula, climbing out of the abyss will seem to be an impossible task. If we're helped by an outside force then it's that force that becomes stronger, rather than ourselves.

This book considers some concepts that have come into my field of vision since writing *On The Other Hand*. The more we focus on and become aware of how our mind works, the more insights we get - only we choose which of these we want to listen to or implement in our lives. The more we focus on and are aware of our difficulties, the more those difficulties continue to be a negative influence and therefore, destructive. It's necessary to continually remind ourselves to turn around when our thoughts wander back to our old ways, but all we need to do when this happens is reconnect to the new ways; with practise, as with everything, we get much better at staying in power.

I decided to illustrate this book with a character I designed for no other reason other than I enjoy creating them and wanted to share them with you. I call this character Dilly (which means something or someone remarkable). Dilly is a 'thought form' that thinks and he shows off some of our most endearing human traits. At present, he'll only appear in the paperback versions of this book.

A Bit of a Rant

We speak sweet intentions, but our
hearts remain silent.

Earlier in this book I wrote about social media and some of the effects it has on our society. Since then I've given it a lot of thought, and it occurs to me that social media isn't sociable at all - it's asocial. In my experience, these 'social' sites are used increasingly to spread, amongst other things, inspirational quotes - a sort of pick 'n' mix philosophy that comes from a variety of sources from the ancient Greeks to modern day 'life coaches'. We don't spread our *own* inspiration or speak our own words of wisdom. I don't say these quotes should stop; I'm saying let's discuss them in a meaningful way rather than just clicking on a 'like' button and treating them like a piece of art we hang on our 'walls'. Some of these quotes have thousands of likes but only a handful of comments; in what way are we inspired, or inspiring, when we do this? On the whole, inspirational quotes have become the junk mail of social media and its presence is only exceeded by advertising. So many quotes are distributed that their potency and original beauty are greatly diluted and therefore, devoid of meaning and quickly forgotten. I asked a girl, who posts these as though they were confetti, if she can remember what she posted the previous day. Her answer was 'No'. I've had to unfollow quite a few people simply because there's no other way to stop the spam. As if it weren't enough that we're being spammed by advertisers, businesses and scams, we're now spamming our family and friends.

What happens when one of our friends persistently posts things we don't want to see? There are three choices - 'unfriend' the person, delete the posts, or put up with them; whichever choice you make there are bound to be consequences of one type or another. I had a friend who introduced me to her new boyfriend and we became good friends - we all knew each other personally. When she decided to end her relationship with him a year later, she said I should end my friendship with him. I refused, and she was very upset about it, saying that I wasn't a good friend to her. I didn't go further into this drama of hers, or agree to be a go-between passing messages between the two online; needless to say she and I are no longer friends. To me we couldn't have been such good friends in the first place. Humanity can be so silly and immature; during my lifetime I've heard more wisdom from children than I have from adults - it's time for humanity to grow up.

A contact of mine on one of these sites said in a post 'smart phones have made this world a lonelier place' and this is partly true. It's not the phones that have made the world into a lonelier place to live in, but our agreement to live our lives through them - they're a technical accessory to the human mind. Phones can't bring people together, as we must be apart in order to use them. Now we meet in game chat rooms and online messaging platforms -

mostly, having no idea with whom we're interacting; it's strictly persona to persona. Instead of friends in real life we've friends on contact lists who we'll probably never meet. The more we frequent social sites the more asocial we become and the more the 'cloud' becomes filled with the phenomenal confusion of our minds; it will never make sense, so there's no point in trying to make sense of it. It's important to see that the cloud is a collective reflection of the mind of humanity - not looking too good right now. Recognising this, goes a long way to finding peace of mind, because we can then walk away without withdrawal symptoms and not rely on a 'cloud' for company or approval. That doesn't mean we have to stop using it - it means we don't have to be online every moment, just in case we miss something that leaves us out of 'the know'.

Technology keeps humanity apart, rather than bringing it together. The internet has become our 'cloak of invisibility' and only *we* choose when, or which masks we don when we're online. We can hide or lay low and choose who goes into which type of friend group, but it's important to see that for each friend group we put on a different mask - we're never complete when we do that. Another tricky part to this is that we hide the parts we like about ourselves the least, so, just as we don't know who we're really talking to, neither do the people we chat with - our screens are always in-between us. At the very least a need to lay low must mean that we don't trust everyone on our friends list in which case, why do we keep them? Some of us have multiple accounts that flicker between visible and invisible modes like fairy lights on a Christmas tree. To bring this into the light, think about how well we know the people we communicate with online; in most cases we don't know if they smoke, how tall they are or if they really live in the country they claim to live in. We don't tend to ask these questions of people online, or even converse with them, and we can't confirm that the picture they put on their profile is actually them, or recent for that matter - it might even be a bot. All we know about these 'friends' is what we've read on their walls - creating the image they want us to form of them - and that's about it. The internet is a place for a meeting of minds, predominantly unhealthy ones. There are more stealth observers on social media websites than there are active participants. If you want proof of this just look at anyone's page who has a reasonable number of friends and see how many actually post.

Mask off   Mask on

Too often we broadcast information, but don't receive it; I've had some 'private' chats with people who keep on typing - message after message - despite my requests that they pause so that I can respond to their original comment. We don't see the person we're talking to as human - people type at us, rather than to us. More often than not we're interested in our own world and don't want to read what anyone else has written. We try to out-do and compete with each other. So social media is a place to broadcast to the masses rather than to an individual and also a place where family members can keep up-to-date with each other. Nothing on these sites is personal or private, yet it's also both. Even if we keep our personal life quiet there's a good chance that someone else may talk about us or post our embarrassing photographs on their page or stealth private groups. Fear of this keeps us from being open and honest because we're always suspicious and *en garde*. We're becoming more and more like the people in E. M. Forster's short story *The Machine Stops* (1909), as we increasingly withdraw from the outside world into our rooms where we spend a great deal of time in front of screens with little to no physical contact. Yes, the internet was *predicted* that far back, before we even had radios let alone televisions. We've become the slaves to the servant we created and we're not looking for our freedom.

Ironically, humanity, long separated, is coming together as One; it's a highly controlled and confused One. It's a depraved One and we created it. It's a One made up entirely of the contents of our minds, which are extremely unhealthy: it's a wireless One. In other words, it removes the need for human physical touch and interaction - it lacks heart. Will future generations be able to read body language at all, or will we be reduced to a 'Swiss army knife' of emoticons on a stick, should we one day meet face to face? The internet can also be used for good. I use it to promote my books in order to raise even just one question in the minds of those who, like me, are curious about their existence or confused about the world we live in. I say I use it to promote my books, but those who know me personally know I don't go too far with that; I'd make a lousy salesperson as I simply don't care enough about it. I trust that those who're meant to read my books will find them; I trust in our universe and I know that none of us are alone. We're all guided and that means you too.

The internet is a fabulous way to reach out, and all conceivable information can be found on it - finding it is just a question of knowing where to look and entering the correct keywords. We can search online for violence or pornographic material and millions of results are found. We can also search for something more meaningful like how humanity could live better lives. Then, proceeding with caution through the abundance of misleading and immature information, it's possible to find little gems that lead to profound changes in our lives. The problem is not the internet - it's the mental health of the people that use it. The internet is the largest library in the world, and in it we've got access to everything we've ever known on this earth - it's also the largest hiding place. There's a great deal on the internet that's healthy for us, and a great deal that isn't - the problem is choice.

Just Around the Bend

We're waiting for miracles that in our hearts we know won't arrive - we have to make them happen.

The wonders of the universe are so far away and beyond our comprehension - the stars, other galaxies and God(?) We're unable to reach up to touch them, but are still fascinated and frustrated by the skies, because we don't actually have a clue about what's 'out there'. We also hope that whatever we find will be better than we have here. An individual can't build their own rocket to go into outer space in order to take a closer look - they can only accept the selected images that are publicised - and hope that one day they'll mean something to them. Closer to home, good health, happiness, peace on earth and a debt-free life appear to be unattainable for our generation - this is the case for our children too. Let me try to put this into perspective; we're so many billions of people living on a planet that in universal or cosmic terms is less than the size of a speck of dust. We don't know who we are or what our purpose is, yet we run around trying to achieve something called 'success' before our exit into oblivion, heaven or the 'hot place' (you may have some other favourite). We leave chaos in our wake, while waiting for either a miraculous phenomenon to occur, or the arrival of a saviour to put the world to rights - we ignore the odds against these.

No wonder there's so much anguish in this world and no visible hope for our future; we immerse ourselves in the world of films, games and social media; in so many ways they're distractions from our lives and seemingly more interesting. However, they're about as much use to our awareness as a key is without a lock - they're just some of the tools of aberration and procrastination, or to put it another way, they keep us living in ignorance, superstition and fear. The distractions, because we focus so strongly on them, silence the mind as long as we remain engrossed - they're therapy, which is any activity that relieves tension. However, when we stop the mind is noisy again which results in us wanting to go back to the games or whatever distraction is our own particular favourite. We participate in these feel-good-pastimes whether it's by savouring a freshly-brewed cup of coffee, eating chocolate or parading down a high street in a new outfit. Whatever leisure activities we choose, even a noisy rave party, they temporarily release us from our incessant mind chatter. When we find ways to quieten the mind we make them habitual.

When we put all this together with the fact that every human being suffers or has suffered in some way, it's no surprise that we don't want to look inside ourselves - each one of us knows what we've buried so deeply. Understanding the mind of humanity is as complicated and mysterious as understanding the universe. We agree to wait in hope for the future because we can't see how this world or our lives have any worthwhile purpose with things the way they are - there's nothing to gain other than more money or more bills. In general, we get little to no job satisfaction because there's none to be had. Most of our jobs are mundane, mechanical and meaningless. The only result that can come out of a world like this is that more and more people become ill, depressed and increasingly unable to cope with their lives - yet still we wait for a brighter future that's always, just around the bend. Considering the above, we're waiting for miracles that no-one believes in. We can't even *see* the bend, let alone around it.

What we're actually waiting for can vary such as birthdays, anniversaries, Christmas, appointments, annual bonuses, change or retirement. Sometimes we're so keen for them to arrive that we prepare in advance like shopping for Christmas four months earlier, or saving money for our old age; ultimately, we're fine-tuning our deaths before thinking about why we're alive. Instead of living our lives purposefully we're waiting for someone else to improve them for us, like governments or an inspirational speaker / author. If we want to live in a peaceful world we have to work together to raise consciousness; we're One. Let's consider happiness, instead of misery.

A great deal of humanity's time is spent waiting for the future to arrive - our whole lives - but it never arrives and it never will. It can't arrive for one good reason; the future doesn't exist and therefore, the bend is infinite. We wouldn't queue today to catch a boat arriving next week. We're queuing to live and don't realise that there's only Now. We're queuing up a dead-end waiting for someone else to bring this impossible future to us; science, governments, help books, super heroes and the like. For some strange reason we believe they'll succeed in doing it one day, if not for us then for our children. However, what we actually get is another version of something technical like a bigger, wider, flatter or higher resolution screen, a new artificial flavour or a promise of a cure for cancer in the future. It's barely enough to build up hopes, and doesn't warrant the trust we put in these authorities. All too often we're 'running on the spot' and one day leads into another that isn't very different from the last. Long term, we're rushing to beat the clock, with no idea where we're going and we're allowing ourselves to be entertained while we're doing it.

I once had a dream that took me a few years just to begin to fathom. In it, a voice said 'We're multi-dimensional time travellers'. How is this possible? The future and past exist only in our minds. Only the future can exist on a working clock face as no clock is accurate enough to pinpoint the Now; just like us the clock's hands chase a future they'll never reach - time obscures the Now until the clock stops ticking. The future exists in our imagination - in pictures of a paradise island and in promises of a stress-free existence when we no longer have to work. For the majority of people this couldn't be further from the truth; for some, the greatest bonus is the privilege of free transport passes and a secure retirement home. The past also is only a thought; we live in the past when we dwell on it and the longer we dwell on it the deeper its roots go and the more venomous its poison. Sure there are happy memories too, but the mind is only interested in drawing our attention to the less positive ones. The future and past are thought forms; we wait for the future and remember the past so what precisely are we doing *Now*? If this makes any kind of sense to you then you'll understand when I say that the mind can be seen as a 'time machine'. The contents of the mind are thoughts from our pasts and hopes for our future and we spend our lives collecting and remembering these - thought is never in the Now. We learnt to remember the past and to look forward to the future. How did we lose the Now?

I had an experience many years ago that I couldn't understand, and it couldn't be explained. It was one afternoon after having had a light general anaesthetic and a laparoscopy; I was taking a nap at home, and painkillers. I dreamt I was in my bed and a large picture with a three-inch picture frame around it fell from its hook onto the floor. I leant over in bed to see the damage and the safety glass had cracked in one corner, but not too badly. The room in my dream was exactly the same as the room I was sleeping in. The picture had hung on the wall for four years. Now, this is where my experience gets interesting. I was startled by the dream and woke up. As I lifted my head from the pillow I watched a repeat of the whole event - even the crack was the same. I've never repaired the picture. The future is not something we can wait for and incredibly, I watched the same event twice. I don't need this experience to be analysed. Drugs can cause tricks of the mind but *this* trick can't be explained in any way that would satisfy me. This happened; I was the only witness and was so excited that I spent over two hours on the phone telling friends all about it - of course no one really believed me. People have doubts when something strange happens to someone else, but not when it happens to them - *no-one* can convince us otherwise. When you know, *you know*, and you can never turn your back on it.

There's something wonderful waiting for us just around the bend - but we don't want to see it. We put off self-realisation - mostly because we think we have time on our side, but we can never have time on our side. Time brings wrinkles and infirmity - not revelations. A young lady once ask me 'How much time do I have here?' How much easier our lives would be if we knew answers to questions like that - perhaps we might think twice about procrastination. We find and defend every excuse to continue with things the way they are; like 'I want to change, but I was hurt, so I can't'. We put up barriers in order to prevent our 'progress'. I put progress in inverted commas because there really is no such thing when it comes to realising who we are. We've nothing at all to learn. Living this life is rather like wandering around a forest looking for something we haven't lost. We can't understand this until we find it. Yes I know this doesn't make complete sense at the moment, but it does when we realise that what we're looking for is not outside but *inside*. Imagine looking out of your lounge window all your life without ever knowing what was in the lounge.

We're already everything we'll ever be, but pretend otherwise. The same young lady (mentioned above) asked me what advice I could give her, so I suggested she observe her mind and find out how it works. She said 'Yes okay, but the observing is hard' and 'I keep myself busy so I don't *have* to think'; this is like calling for help when drowning, but sending away the lifeboat when it arrives. The road to revelation has no bargain basements, no special offers and no group workshops; the work isn't easy, I know, but we can each of us do it if we're serious. We ask 'how can we observe our mind', but in my experience we really don't want to. What we *really* want is to be given confirmation that we *can't* do it; we're looking for a sick-note, so we don't have to be an active participant in raising our consciousness level; we want our 'advisor' to be responsible for our journey, so that *we* don't have to be - in other words, we're skiving. Society is pampered and lazy. It doesn't want change if it has to work for it and it doesn't want to make sacrifices. We want everything delivered to our doorsteps just like our takeaways and shopping. We're not on *our* path to self-realisation when we're dependent on others to show us the way - we're on someone else's and who knows where that will lead.

If we're everything that ever was, or ever will be, why can't we just know it now? In truth, because we don't want it badly enough and put it off for as long as we can; we think we're in control of our lives, but this is so far from the truth. We don't even 'play it safe' - well a few do, but mostly we'd prefer our place to be reserved while we look elsewhere; we like to keep our options open. Here are a few excuses we make to prevent ourselves seeing the truth about our world:

- I'll do it tomorrow.
- I've got a full-time job.
- I've lots of mouths to feed.
- I want to, but I just don't have the time.
- It's alright for you …

Do any of these sound like familiar excuses? These are all arguments put forward by the mind. We're afraid to look around the bend because we're not sure what's there (if anything at all) and the mind keeps us afraid for as long as we allow it to. Just around the bend can seem too far away and too much effort to reach. Going around the bend is an insecure experience and this is a key reason why we don't do it; for some strange reason we believe we've something to lose, like our sanity. We don't want to take chances that we can't guarantee will pay off and there's no complaints department, should things not pan out as we'd like them to - it's a leap of faith. So we bide our time hoping someone will keep *our* seat free for us on the next boat. In other words, we let others do the work, such as scientists or politicians as though they were capable of finding a shortcut and we become their silent audience. The mind is like our car - either our hands are on the wheel or they're not, in which case it'll collide with something sooner or later, unless we take back control of it.

$\sim\sim\sim$

Do you really believe you're an irrelevant reject of this universe? Two important questions we can ask ourselves are 'Have I reached the highest height I'm capable of reaching' and 'Do I put my heart and soul into the things I want to achieve'. If you answer 'Yes' to either of these, then why are you reading this book? It can be of no use to you. If you answer 'No' to them - well, recognising this is a great step forward, as it were.

The more we delay what we all know innately we must get on with sooner or later, the more our shame and guilt build up. The effect on our health and stress levels are horrendous. I declared to my partner that I was going to stop smoking in exchange for a new laptop. He was looking at them online and called me over to look at a particularly interesting one. I said 'I'd stop smoking for that' and we went out the same day and he bought it for me. Now I was in a bit of a pickle because I'd made a promise and the present didn't feel like a good time to fulfil it - I quite enjoyed smoking. It took me six months to prepare for the mental marathon and after that time, with only two cigarettes left in my packet, I told him I wouldn't buy any more. He doubted me and I don't blame him. He said 'you'll want some later this evening, so we better buy a packet just in case' but I stood my ground and said 'No. These two are the last two'. I smoked and enjoyed them and threw the empty packet into the bin - I've not touched another one since. The guilt I felt over the six months grew and grew and more so because he never mentioned it or reminded me of my promise. The relief I felt after stopping was amazing and I was never tempted to start again. When we put our minds to something and really want to achieve it, we're almost there; the next step is to put the plan into action and then keep our eye on the goal.

Because of our inertia we can't collectively see beyond this reality, but I can assure you this reality is temporary and transitive. Whatever we do has consequences and whatever decisions we make in this life are our responsibility. We can't always see the results of our actions, but that doesn't mean they don't exist. We have to leave this world empty handed - the same way we arrived. Now is the only time to think about what we're doing here, and whether we've enough time to complete it. Humanity is heading somewhere and carrying a tremendous and heavy burden with it. Each one of us can lighten that burden by observing ourselves closely and not passing our grievances and foolishness on for the next generation to sort out. Nothing in this world is worth holding on to, nor is it possible to take it with us when we die. Those who do decide to look further into their minds and question their own dogmas, are mostly considered to be out of touch with reality. Overcoming this criticism may well prove to be the greatest obstacle - it depends on whether you care about the judgement of others or not.

As long as there's a need for approval and a consensus to live in fear, we can't see the world as it truly is. By abdicating our responsibility and putting our trust in other people, we agree to be controlled by them doing what they think is best for us, or rather for *them*. Society doesn't encourage individuality or the questioning of its rituals, rather, it encourages inertia in these matters. We sponsor and commercialise physical strength, beauty, acting ability and wealth, applauding them with awards of one sort or another. But, when a person sees through the charade and wants to change this world into a happier and more loving place to live in, we label them a 'bad influence'; *this* is insanity.

Scotty? Beam me up!

Completeness

*When we stop looking
for help, we realise we
never needed any.*

As a child I was obsessed with the idea of dying and wanted to do so before I reached the age of thirty. Death didn't frighten me at all - I'd become used to the idea through recurrent dreams in which I died - although I did feel fear of the method. Thirty seemed very old to me - it was 'grown-up' and every grown up I'd ever known had been unkind, indifferent or hypocritical towards me; the last thing I ever wanted to be was a grown up. I was fifteen when struck with an insane idea. My family were gathered around the dinner table and as usual, raising their voices at each other - in French - so I'd no idea what they were fighting about and they didn't seem to notice that my sister and I were even in the room - we were invisible and always had been. I left the room unnoticed, went to the bathroom and gathered all the painkillers I could find - there were plenty. I took them up to my bedroom with a couple of glasses of water and sat down in front of my dressing table. One by one I swallowed them, counting them out loud, until I'd taken forty. I felt no fear or emotion, but imagined that this act would bring out some sort of emotion in my father - a change of heart. I left the house and went to the nearest phone booth to call the only friend I had, and told him what I'd done. He took me to the hospital. I still felt no fear or emotion. The stomach pump wasn't fun at all - I rather hated the experience, but harder to swallow was the reaction of my father. He arrived at the hospital, at their request, sat down by my bedside and wrote me a cheque for £50. He handed it to me saying 'buy something to cheer yourself up' and left. I felt as flat as the cheque now lying on my bedside locker. This wasn't how it was supposed to end at all and, apart from a short visit from a doctor to assess my mental state the following morning, no-one ever mentioned the incident again. At this point in my life - and for many years following - I believed I needed my father's love to make me complete. I never got it so unconsciously sought it elsewhere.

~~~

Divorce and re-marriage are the acceptable norm and a divorcee is often regarded as being 'back on the market'; what a strange term. Blinded by confusion, I was insecure, naïve and searching for a dream - unaware it was only an illusion. My only purpose was to get married, have children and not to make the same mistakes my parents made - putting my children into an orphanage. I married many times because I was unable to discern then what I see clearly now. Foolishly, I believed I could right the wrongs of the past. To believe that something from the outside could make me complete meant I saw myself as *incomplete*. I was searching for a 'normal' family in order to become part of a *whole*, rather than a fragment, but this search is a diversion from what really needs to be done. I wanted to be a better parent to my children than my parents had been to me; this is like looking for a future that can change our past. It's also looking for someone to fulfil our dreams for us and holding up a flag that says 'Rescue Me'.

This is the life we've been encouraged to strive for through 'happily ever after' films and stories. I was searching for my fairytale-ending before I'd even begun to live. The fantasy became an obsession and I thought about nothing else. I'd no ambitions other than to live in a doll's house, walk through the door wearing a white wedding dress and to have my own front door key to lock the world out - letting someone else take responsibility for me. What I didn't know then is that I was locking myself in. When things inevitably went wrong, I quickly found a replacement crutch to lean on, because I was afraid to be alone. The marital vow 'till death do us part' has lost its importance for most of us and perhaps should be replaced by 'until I wake up' and realise there are no knights in shining armour, no princesses to save, no short-cuts to self-knowledge and no-one who can carry us to our *Self*.

Never think more of someone than you think of yourself. When we fall for someone, we tend to ignore their shortfalls (or view them as endearing) so that in the rush of romance they appear to be our ideal partner. I now see this as insanity driven by irrational need. We need someone else to be solid for us, to hold our hand, give meaning to our life and give us what we think we lack. In order to live with our *flaws* rather than our *strengths* we look up to someone, creating a symbiotic relationship, but we're not aware we're doing it - it's a survival instinct. What we're really trying to do is *join* ourselves to someone else, but two people can't make each other complete or fill the void in each other's lives. We do it because if we didn't put our hope in others, we'd have to face ourselves.

By looking up to someone else, we place ourselves beneath them. This gives us an excuse to stay exactly where we want to be and they become our *prop* - we surrender to them. The pedestal we've stood them on is constructed from need and desire. In much the same way we look to society to be this 'prop' and get comfort from being a part of something bigger than ourselves - we play a passive role. Deep in our hearts we know that the key to our freedom lies 'within' and the reason we don't admit to it, is because we're not ready to be self-contained.

By finding people we believe need our help or can help us, we somehow feel worthwhile and it avoids us taking a long hard look at ourselves for the more esoteric questions that may give meaning to our lives. What we're really looking for is a distraction from the stresses in our everyday life. If fairy tales are to be believed then in order to live happily ever after, we must find our prince or princess; this only gives us an excuse to believe that our happiness hasn't arrived yet, because of some misfortune. The reality is that these relationships are deep in work, dirty dishes, children, nappies, paying bills, stress, frustration and being able to fluently converse on cultural and 'soap opera' current affairs. Problems arise because just as we want to continue with the *status quo*, so do the people we find. In other words, they don't want to change any more than we do. Initially the relationship feels energised because we've 'balanced' ourselves, but it's only a matter of time before the batteries run down and we realise the truth; we're still incomplete and our companion doesn't have our missing pieces.

We want to be with a new partner twenty four hours a day and if the relationship is based on symbiotic need, sooner or later we'll want to be as far away from each other as possible. This is one of the reasons relationships can become stale; nothing actually changes because we're relying on someone else to make those changes for us. Think of it as two people sitting either end of a see-saw - they're dependent on each other and if one gets off, then the other comes crashing down. However, if a couple find completeness in themselves, rather than each other, they'll stand a good chance of having a healthy and progressive relationship. A relationship in which two roses can bloom side-by-side.

Why do we need to look up to someone else to make us complete? This is a question of faith, but it's a false faith. What we actually look for is our shadow - that which we're afraid to claim as ourselves, which is why we externalise our search. The person we find is doing the same thing - they also feel incomplete. A shadow is not necessarily dark - it's the parts of us that we deny existence to. Someone content to live a wicked life has a light shadow; he knows he's not living in his highest interest, but never listens to that inner voice. However, we're only window shopping and the shop front will always keep us separated. Let me explain this a little more. We're on one side of the glass looking into the shop for what we think we need. What we believe we need is looking straight back at us. So why isn't it a perfect match? Because it's not really us. It's part of somebody else. We already have what we're looking for to make us complete but we're (1) in denial of that and (2) unwilling to confirm it by taking a look. This is an insecurity. We think so little of ourselves that it seems impossible that we're all we ever need. Just as in our high streets, it's in these shop windows that desire is born and this desire can never bear fruit that won't one day rot. One tree can't bear the fruit of another. We see what we want to see, listen for the words we want to hear and only accept that which suits our agenda.

It's also for these reasons that we choose to ignore the mischief of governments. There isn't a soul who doesn't know that governments are corrupt, dysfunctional and never stick to their manifesto promises. They bring poverty, misery, illness, war and neglect to the people they govern. Despite this knowledge we choose to mechanically re-elect them to govern our world. We do this for several reasons including fear, laziness and insecurity - yet few will admit to that. We look to them to do what we believe we can't, yet we know full well they can't either.

~~~

Often we turn our attention to celebrities and see what we want to see via the various forms of media and social interaction outlets. We ignore any notion that the images we have of these icons have been created by others - they're faux. The characters Clint Eastwood plays in the spaghetti westerns are good examples of this; we're led to believe they're tough, indestructible and in complete control of their lives. However, this image is an on-screen image and not the character of the actor off-screen. As a small child I turned my attention to David Cassidy though I'd no idea who he was. I listened to his songs, *I Think I Love You* and *Daydreamer* again and again, imagining I was good enough to be the girl he was singing to - getting lost in the illusion. But it wasn't because I wanted his life - it was because I didn't like my own and because according to the lyrics, he understood me. Listening to his songs gave me temporary relief from what was then, an incredibly noisy mind. It's also about energy - he had it and I didn't and by mimicking him, I felt some of that energy. This is one of the reasons there are so many copycat and lookalike artists in the world - they haven't found their own purpose / skill. The same principle applies when we copy fashion and other trends shown to us through celebrities or advertising campaigns.

When we look closer at what's happening here we see that we only see snapshots of successful people's lives and then wear their names on T-Shirts, or model ourselves on them. We become the character's 'fan' because we feel a void in our own lives and in some odd way they fill it, by proxy. This is an illusion and if the actor so much as trips over a pebble in real life the illusion is either destroyed or ignored. If ignored we continue to believe and make excuses for their momentary lapse and if destroyed, we seek someone else to take their place. Characters on-screen are powerful and influential in our lives, regardless of whether they're villains or heroes and this is true in blockbuster films or the more minor, but no less influential, soap operas. We can't see that the actors are just like us; we see what we want to see, hear what we want to hear and make them into our gods. Like in dreams, we must one day wake up and realise that what we believe to be real, isn't. The word 'fan' is derived from 'fanatic' - that's got to be worth pondering. Following someone else's habits and behaviours is rather like reading someone's book and then writing our name over theirs - plagiarising someone's life. We've our own book to write. We all have the ability to be creative but we don't believe we can do it, even though we do it every moment of our lives.

If someone tries to tell us the truth about the person we glorify, we don't want to know and put up a huge amount of resistance in order to reinforce our beloved delusions. This is true even if the person we're glorifying tells it to us and refuses to accept our irrational inflated opinions of them. Placing someone on a pedestal they're unable to stand on causes problems in relationships; the relationship is based on a false notion and the pedestal will crack under the pressure. Because of this it can never bring peace or happiness, other than of a temporary nature. The situation will always require a victim and someone to be their saviour, who is also incomplete - they need someone to *save* and believe they can do it.

The delusion is more wide-angled than it seems at first glance. On its lowest level it's where a person may choose to remain in an abusive relationship. We often believe we can't survive without the person involved and keep going under the delusion that things will change one day. In a lot of cases we're convinced we're responsible for our partner's behaviour. Why? Because they convinced us of it. By claiming responsibility for someone else's behaviour we're making excuses for them - it's a small price to pay and it serves both parties. This is an evasive tactic we make in order not to take responsibility for ourselves - it's our albatross. On its highest level the delusion requires the worship of an outside and invisible force, such as any one of the variety of gods we worship (metaphysical or physical). Somewhere in-between lay our relationships with our employers, friends and other family members.

There are people who choose to remain where they are in life, and continue making the same mistakes, and there are those who seek them out in order to play out what they enjoy most - control. There are also people who feel an irresistible urge to break the glass and walk away from the destructive and repetitive patterns in their lives. You're one of those, because you're reading this now. More often than not the root causes of this behaviour are irrational fear and apathy. Deep down we already know all we need to know about ourselves and those we come into contact with. If we look closely at our own thoughts we see that we push aside the wise ones in favour of the reckless. Because we don't believe we can survive by ourselves, trust we put in outside forces must, by definition, be misplaced. We put trust in other people to do what we feel unable to do ourselves. A strong character attracts a weaker one, but if we look carefully it's easy to see that the weaker character is in complete control; without the consent of a 'weaker' character to dominate, a strong character has no power. Generally speaking, 'weaker' characters are only weak because they've *forgotten* their own strengths, preferring not to remember them because then, they'd have to take responsibility for themselves. It's this way with society too.

We're dissatisfied with ourselves and hope that someone stronger will save us by whisking us away to a place of safety - anyone will do, as long as it's not us. We've also been taught to think that solutions to problems in our lives lie in things like large bank accounts - measurements of our success. Not true? How many people buy lottery tickets, and how many people buy more than one? By looking up to people who've apparently cracked the problem we can make more excuses about why we can't, by putting their good fortune down to luck or talent. We look up to people who have, or can achieve, what *we* can't, and set them up as our role models, but this mindset is twisted because we can never become them. We set ourselves up to fail and rely on outside forces to stimulate us. It's a way of living our lives through something or somebody else and its root is apathy.

When we look outside for help or completeness, we also look outside for someone to blame when things go wrong in our lives: we want someone to be responsible and someone who can alleviate our pain and suffering. The most obvious example of this is that we leave the world in the hands of the politicians and corporations - then blame *them* because we're not living in a Garden of Eden - conveniently forgetting that we vote them into power and buy the carrots they dangle in front of us. However, when we're in the driving seat - instead of the 'mind' or a government - there's no need for any adjustment or remedy. There's no need for gender categorisation labels either; weak, strong, housewife or hero; there's no need to try to become something we're not. The only thing we need to *become* is who we already are. We're not fragments but over time we've become 'fragmented'; we're already complete and we only need to realise this. We started believing we're incomplete because we allowed ourselves to be convinced of it, by society. Through vigilance and the observance of our own mind and behaviour, we realise that we're not incomplete at all.

Mind Dramas

Yesterday has already happened - we don't have to re-master, splice, edit or re-live it.

Every moment we process information picked up from a variety of sources. On a physical level the sources include teachers, media outlets, books, friends, acquaintances and family. This information is then processed through our personal filters, according to our bias and conditioning. It's not until we step back and think about what's happening that the process becomes apparent. The actions of others pull triggers that appeal to, upset or offend us - they also create fear. Whatever our reaction, its roots lie in our past experiences and we allow them to create what becomes a smash-hit drama, in which we're starring. The root of these dramas is often that we don't feel good enough - we feel unworthy and therefore, insecure. The dramas become *real* and set in motion a chain of events producing emotions and reactions that validate them. Our dreams have the same effect on us. I remember once waking with my partner in the morning and he'd felt annoyed that I'd smoked a cigarette, after having recently given them up - but this was just the residual thoughts and feelings from his dream. Nevertheless, the emotions were real for him and though he *knew* I hadn't smoked, he'd found it hard to ignore his dream. Our dreams can seem so real that when we wake up from them we react as though we were really *there* and participating in the storyline. Nightmares from my childhood were exactly like that, and in one recurring dream I used to wake up just as I was being shot. I awoke in a cold sweat with a tight pain in my chest - symptoms of fear or dread, as though it had really happened.

We've been creating the dramas for so long now that we don't realise we're doing it - we absorb the effects like emotional sponges. Take for example watching a film in the cinema. Our reactions to scenes in the film depend on the genre and include, but aren't limited to sadness, remorse, anger, fear, disgust, revelation, shock, horror, compassion and hope. Yet, all we did to bring about these reactions was buy a ticket and take our seat. Nothing happened to us, personally, and we haven't interacted with anyone off-screen. The drama isn't real - it's information from sounds and images perceived by our senses. It's happening in our mind - a hard concept to grasp initially but when it falls into place we wonder how we never noticed it before. We literally, during some scenes, sit on the edge of our seats in fear or anticipation (sometimes both) as the action grips our senses dragging us into the reality of the film as though we were participating in it.

One of the most famous scenes that terrified audiences worldwide was the shower scene in the film *Psycho* (1960), where the character played by Janet Leigh met her end. Auditory and visual memories from this scene remain in our minds. Proof that this happens is that I still remember them now and if you know the film, so do you - they're embedded. There were reports that some people apparently feared getting into their showers after watching *Psycho*. Sound and vision were used to produce the same effect in the film *Jaws* (1975) but instead of dreading a shower, many people feared swimming in the sea after watching it. Our reactions to scenes like these are far stronger when we watch the evolving three-dimensional films because they're more realistic. Sometimes our reactions are so strong that, when we get back home, we double check we've locked all the doors and windows. Why do we like these self-induced fear experiences? Perhaps it's because we survive them and walk out of the cinema unscathed. Perhaps it's because our mind errs on the negative side of life. We enjoy the terror and fear, which is why these films and others like them are produced more and more; demand equals supply. Humanity has become disconnected from what they see in such films - our minds don't see the long-term effects that permeate so deeply into society; such as ignorance, apathy and complacency.

The more we watch such films, the more our reactions to the violence or sex in them are neutralised. Many children watch these films with no *apparent* ill effects and without this content, they'd find them boring and passive. They watch these films from a younger and younger age and when they're not watching them, they get the same *information* from books and games they download. Imagine showing a child an episode of the 1950s / 1970s *Dixon of Dock Green* series today. Its slow and comparatively mild-mannered pace wouldn't hold their attention - it isn't scary or exciting enough.

We crave the fast-paced action-packed content for entertainment which matches the increasingly fast-paced and limited perspective of our lives. Consequently, the dramas playing in our minds are just as fearful and fast-paced off-screen as on. We end up not being able to understand the mess and confusion in our minds, as much as we can't understand it in the world; we live in fear and perhaps the biggest fear of all is to be in *silence* - we don't know *how* to be silent. For most people silence means loneliness, but this loneliness is really a fear of being left alone with only our mind for company. I know now that loneliness is an inability to live with our shadow; the noise inside that knows us so well - when we're alone we can't hide from it. The mind forces us to focus on things we'd rather not focus on (ourselves) and it's for this reason we like to keep busy with work, leisure, play, social media, television programmes and music. The louder the noise we can make around us, the less we hear our mind and the less we hear ourselves.

We love extreme drama. We live in fear but we also love the experience of that fear, which is why we love roller-coaster rides and other 'scaries'. There's a ride at the Stratosphere Tower in Las Vegas called *Insanity* that spins people round a mechanical arm at a height of 900 feet, generating 3 'G's. Scarier still is a ride called *Big Shot* at the same tower that generates an experience of 4 'G's and as if that wasn't enough you can now be thrust 30 feet over the building at 30mph, if you so choose. There's plenty of people who want to go on these rides. These so called 'thrill' rides have become more and more terrifying and there's a great demand for them. But we don't enjoy these things just because of an adrenaline hit. What we love most of all is that while we're being terrified, in that moment, we're not thinking about our daily worries. While we're being thrust off a building we're not thinking about relationships, bills, work, mowing the lawn or anything else. We're living carefree right inside that moment - the Now.

Less extreme, are dramas like finding the courage to chat up someone at a club or other social venue - though some people may well prefer to be launched off the Stratosphere Tower at 30mph. Somewhere in between there's going for an interview, going to the dentist or standing in a queue at a supermarket checkout getting irate because the cashier is idly chatting while our frozen produce melts. Many other dramas pass through our minds while we're waiting in queues; the mind loves the opportunity to get our full attention. This is particularly true in traffic jams and some of these have miles of tailbacks. Why do queues affect us? Because we temporarily have no choice but to be still and think while we wait; we've no control and our mind seizes the opportunity to create dramas that occupy us. The word *queue* (15th century) means *tail of a beast* and who could argue with that definition?

Interpersonal relationships are also affected by abstract dramas - mostly imagined. The longer we interact with a person, the more complicated the dramas of our minds regarding them can become. Each interaction reinforces our deep-seated beliefs and prejudices; when you put that alongside our natural tendency to lean towards the *negative*, it's easy to see how resentment builds up - without provocation. For example, let's say that a friend borrowed a book from you six months ago and hasn't returned it. How many times would you run the conversation in your mind about asking for it back, enacting possible outcomes, including ending your friendship? Perhaps you want to forget about it, but your mind won't let you - even in bed as you're trying to sleep it's churning away. Each time you remember it, more resentment builds up. You may feel angry, bitter, rejected or used. Whatever the feelings, they get out of proportion and even permeate your dreams. It's important to realise that you've written a drama and that you're playing and continually rehearsing every part in it, including that of the audience and critics. The chances are your friend is completely unaware of your turmoil and forgotten altogether about the book. A gentle reminder may be all that's needed and your mind will quieten, at least where this subject is concerned. It's far better to have peace of mind than to hold onto a grudge based on an imagined scenario. I remember hearing a joke about a man who wanted to borrow his neighbour's lawnmower and he ran an incredible script through his mind predicting the negative outcome of his request. By the time he knocked on the door and the man answered he said 'You know what ... you can stuff your lawnmower'. This may be a joke, but we do this sort of thing all the time - the mind encourages it. We create the drama out of nothing at all.

There's another drama that plays a part in our lives and that's the long-term random repetitive reminders of past pains and suffering. I call these random because they pop up unexpectedly, while we're doing or thinking about something unconnected. The mind doesn't want us to forget the past and it's constantly reminding us of things; it replays not only the story, but variations of it, even twenty or thirty years after the event. I was haunted for many years by memories of my father, wondering how or what I could do or say that would make him feel differently about me. The more I focused on the situation, the bigger its influence became in my life. As far back as I can remember these painful and damaging thoughts plagued my days and nights; my father was mostly my waking thought and the last one before I went to sleep, which is why he appeared so often in my dreams.

This continued until I was around thirty-five when a psychotherapist explained that I'd given my power to my father; it came as quite a shock to me, because I'd never thought of myself as someone who had had any power to *give* away. I began to take back my power and to see that there were some things in the world I could never change - first and foremost on the list were *other* people. I realised it was possible to change the self-pity, self-hatred, grudges and bitterness that took up so much space in my mind, by taking responsibility for them. I saw that the source of my unhappiness was not my father, but me. I'd discovered that the 'me' I thought myself to be, was in fact a clever and highly manipulative fraud. We too often focus on how other people have hurt us and don't realise that we hurt and judge ourselves far more harshly than anyone else ever could. These dramas hang in frames on the walls of our mind and will remain there until we decide to take them down. The walls we've constructed are reinforced and patrolled by the mind - they're an illusion. We don't have to remain behind them.

~~~

We don't just create our *own* dramas, but jump into other people's productions too, regardless of whether we know them or not. One way we do this is to listen to and spread gossip. Why do we do it? Often because we've nothing better to do and nothing more interesting to say or if we do, no-one who wants to listen to it. Often we want to fit in with the person we're talking to and gossip is what's expected in order to rank highly on someone's popularity list. So we spread the latest *newscast* or fabricate another one and marvel at our ingenuity, despite the mini-drama at the back of our minds that knows we don't feel good about it. I bumped into a neighbour of mine a few months ago and she asked if I'd found my dog. I told her I hadn't lost him and she didn't believe me. 'Oh well,' she puzzled 'I suppose it was someone else's dog', before getting into her car and driving off. So I knew I'd been the subject of gossip and it wasn't long before how it started got back to me. We've become expert at gossip and social media has become an unpleasant extension of it. One of the biggest reasons to gossip about other people is that we're dissatisfied with our own lives and another, that we've nothing better to do; we often find their lives more interesting than our own.

Another way we enjoy other people's dramas is by being an audience. We love soap operas, slowing down to look at accidents on the motorway (rubber-necking), standing around watching an ambulance crew and being kept up-to-date with scandals; we have a morbid curiosity and love to make a drama out of a crisis. Our mind also loves to imagine what people might think about us, even though we haven't done anything wrong; a form of insecurity. One example is how we behave when we're leaving a shop with our purchases and the alarm bells ring. Everyone stares as though we've stolen something and though this is not the case, feelings of shame and embarrassment arise as though we'd *actually* committed the act and these feelings arise because we believe other people think we're guilty. We love to think the worst of people and often what we imagine people think about us isn't true; some of the people staring may simply be feeling relief that it wasn't them that set off the alarms. Why do we care about what people think? It's because we seek approval from outside sources and in this scenario at least, what we get is more like condemnation.

~~~

There are many of us who have a need to bring other people into our drama and this is often at the cost of friendship. This situation arises when someone is so engrossed in their own problems - relationship, health, work or family - that they can't see anything outside their own story. Even a good listener tires of listening to the same boyfriend / girlfriend problems again and again and struggles to hide the fact. The *victim* will use this lack of interest to deepen their 'unworthy' or 'nobody cares' beliefs. I'd suggest that we don't actually *want* anyone to listen or even to give us advice; what we seek is a sounding-board and validation of our right to feel miserable, because we believe the severity of our problem warrants it. If we're given this validation, it confirms the belief that we can't change - this is the pay off.

~~~

Our minds and bodies respond to the information they receive and for this reason it's a good idea to choose what information we 'upload' into them; the information becomes who we think we are and influences how we react to the world around us. The mind recalls memories and therefore, the past. We create our dramas from our memories and only we know the script - no-one else has access to it. One way to stop the noise in our heads is to recognise and watch the thoughts coming and going. Initially this isn't easy as our mind wanders off without us realising it, we daydream or even fall asleep. The thoughts come and go like waves on an ocean but we can choose to surf on them or let them roll to the shore; either way they're still part of the ocean - memories. All too often we catch another wave before the one we're riding on breaks. Sometimes my mind catches me out and I ponder some pointless thoughts for longer than necessary. As soon as I recognise this the thoughts dissolve and I can't find them again; it's a bit like going upstairs to get something and then forgetting what it was I went up there for. However, the mind quickly replaces the thought with another and at first, we need to repeat the process often. The mind is *wild* and arguing with it will prove fruitless - it holds all information about you and knows all your strengths and weaknesses. It can be recognised and observed and with that comes a greater understanding of who we are and why we dwell on so much negativity. With this understanding, the mind quietens and we create fewer, if any, dramas in our lives.

It's possible to stop these dramas once we've set our *intention* to end our pain and suffering. However, in order to work with that intention, vigilance is needed to recognise our 'unhealthy' thought patterns as soon as they manifest. For example, contacting an estranged friend or family member can be a tough beast to conquer. More often than not we can't remember what caused the dispute in the first place, or why it's gone on for so long. Pride and foolishness raise their ugly heads *insisting* we hold on to the grudges but by working in line with our 'intention' we can overcome these when we recognise their familiar faces. Mind dramas are the ego's self-defence mechanisms and its armour is strong, particularly when it senses danger. Stubbornness is nothing more than an impenetrable force-field constructed of fears and it's us who are locked behind it. The only obstacle that prevents us from finding peace is *us*. Our ego controls each one of our masks and it's under the protective custody of the mind. The ego loves role-playing games and it's a Master of Disguise.

Independence

We can depend on not becoming
independent.

Independence is something we strive for without comprehending what it is. Amongst other things, the act of seeking independence is seeking separation from the rest of humanity. Countries fight to become independent, children leave home to become independent and we seek well paid employment so that one day we may achieve this *independence*. These are somewhat illusory goals for no matter what, we live in dependence of *something*. If we didn't, we wouldn't be where we are now. Humanity is separated, but it's also dependent on that separation to keep itself going in the direction it believes it has no choice but to follow - it no longer requires *free will*. If we decide to change course and create a peaceful beautiful world to live in, we'll need each other to do it. Humanity is a team, despite its cells pretending to be individuals and this frame of mind has come about through the coordinated efforts of every one of us. However, whether we like it or not we work together; a nail can't drive itself into the wood and a football can't kick itself into the goal. Even air is dependent on the space it occupies and we're dependent on that air for our next breath. It's only man, in his audacity, who believes otherwise - on some level we all know this is pointless.

We're dependent on the society we've created, and it's dependent on us. Each thing in it exists because of another and they can't be separated; everything and everyone is connected and inter-dependent. You exist because your parents brought you into the world.

- Shops exist because of desires.
- Police exist because of crime.
- Beauty parlours exist because of vanity.
- The poor exist because of the rich.
- Starvation exists because of the greedy.
- Doctors exist because of disease.
- Bullies exist because of victims.

Even excuses exist because of a lack of responsibility. Increasingly, foundations and charities exist because we care only for our own needs - this leaves others to go without. We claim our rights to things we're entitled to, but we've become so self-centred that we care not for those who are unable to claim theirs; instead of supporting them we judge and condemn them. Misery and loneliness exist because of separation - the separation of each and every one of us. Anyone who denies that humanity is separated has forgotten that he's connected to the tramp in the street, the poor, the pitiful and the sorrowful; he's forgotten also that we charge them to live on their own planet. We are One and dependent on each other; the actions of one of us affects the lives of others. Some of these effects are minor and some major - like in wars. We care about ourselves, and not about those who pay the price for our vanities, and we'll continue to do this, all the while charity bridges the gap between us. How come you may ask? Because we're excused from responsibility when we do our bit by dropping our pennies into charity boxes - it doesn't improve the situation if you drop in pounds. If we look at this objectively, it's easy to see that as long as charity exists between us and those in need, people will continue to go without.

Humanity is being willingly driven at high speed to an unknown destination and refusing to consider where it might be going - neither knowing nor caring who the driver is - regardless of the consequences. Humanity blunders on, complaining about the driver's intentions and huffing and puffing at - or blaming - the other passengers for the unfortunate casualties along the way. With nothing more to go on than a tacit agreement between the driver and his passengers to drive where he sees fit - he's been given carte blanche to drive off the edge of a cliff, should he choose to. Yet, despite opportunities to disembark at every stop, humanity chooses to remain on board. The twist in the above analogy is that, long term, the driver doesn't know where he's going either; the driver needs us and we think we need the driver. Taking this analogy to another level - who is this driver? Is anyone at the helm at all, or is the bus being driven by society itself?

Scotty! Do you read me?

~~~

One argument I've heard against the non-existence of independence is 'I'm independent. I go to work, support my family, own my own house, take care of my children and depend on no-one'. This is a specious argument and so easy to dismantle. For one thing, we're dependent on our employers for our salaries, pensions and the continuity of our contract. This argument also shows that you care only for your own agenda and therefore, ignore the needs of the rest of humanity, who belong to this world as equally as you do; it's an 'I'm alright' mentality. Another argument is 'I run my own business'; then you're dependent on your clients, materials, paper, pens, banks and many other things. We're as dependent on society as a child is on its parents; dependence is inescapable for everyone.

Independence = In-*dependence*

A multi-millionaire may seem to be independent but he isn't - far from it; he's less independent than the poverty stricken people in third world countries. Money needs maintenance and he'll need trustworthy staff to manage his life and guard his wealth. Like us, he still needs to eat and drink and more than anything, he's dependent on the silence of the majority to keep him in his privileged position. One of the most difficult things about having money is that we can't let go of it and always want more which in the long run, means more people go without. No matter how much money we accumulate, we still live in pain, uncertainty and a restlessness that's occurred because of our separation.

Look to nature for proof; everything is inter-dependent and that's one of the things that makes it so wonderful - everything needs everything. We too are part of nature and couldn't exist without it, yet have allowed ourselves to become divided in the most insane ways. We'd all like to be independent, and strive for it one way or another. We seek independence because we believe that with it will come this thing called security, but we don't really know what that means. Sure, we can become financially secure, but that won't heal what's hurting inside us and more importantly it won't remove the real sicknesses of our society - fear and apathy being just two of them. Mostly we fear death and in particular, a painful death. Death to each of us is as natural as apples falling from a tree - it will happen.

Even if it were possible to achieve independence, it would be pointless. It would be like the left leg seeking independence from the right. We're connected; each one of us is an essential component in the design of the world that we've created, yet we choose to ignore this fact. We can only function as One, despite our attempts to pretend otherwise. We could achieve what we think of as *freedom*, objectively, by working together - all of us; this planet is rich in food and there's enough to sustain us all. The only difference between the majority and financially secure multi-millionaires, is the size and quality of the cages they live in. The only thing we all *really* need in this world is each other, but for now we have to walk alone, because the crowd aren't ready to see that.

~~~

From a young age we've been subjected to common thoughts and influences. The toys we play with are limiting and designed to help us to fit in with and perpetuate an established and ritualistic society; we learn our ABC's and 123's together with dexterity, physical fitness and hand-eye coordination. Our lives are geared towards becoming independent and in many ways this is a *good* thing, because we *should* be able to stand on our own two feet - taking our allotted places in society; however, this independence is relative and illusory, as no matter how independent we like to think we are, we still depend on so many other things in order that we remain standing; for example, if a person loses their job they look to society to support them until they find another, and without such support they'd fall upon hard times. There are many other examples I could give, and when we start to think about them, we come to realise that we're not at all independent - we're inter-dependent. Understanding this is something, I think, that's missing from our education. We learn all the skills needed to work in either blue or white collar fields. Never are we taught that we can think freely or imaginatively about who we are, where we came from or what we're doing here, or more importantly, where we may be going. Questioning our way of existence is strongly discouraged, and philosophy is rarely part of any curriculum before we're old enough to attend university, if we do at all - for so many years we've been trained to function in a rigid and unrelenting society, on which we're all dependent for our survival.

'What if' and Other Worries

Look to the light and the shadows
will stretch out behind you.

The question 'What if?' is that bucket of water used to quench the fire of joy, inspiration and hope, which we pour over ourselves - or somebody else does it for us. 'What if?' also gives us permission to worry about something that may or may not happen in the future - it's a pre-order for something that doesn't exist. When we give this a little thought we see that it's a self-limiting activity that saps our valuable energy and fills us with inertia.

'What if?' is close to 'but', inasmuch as it's a clause or condition that cancels out rational thought. Before I go any further, I want to make it clear that there are times when 'What if?' is prudent, but these are not the times I'm talking about. I'm referring to those times when we're not genuinely looking for a solution; For example, 'I want to get out more, *but* what if I get hit by a bus?' or 'I want to leave my job, *but* what if I can't find another one?' 'What if?' and 'but' give us our excuses not to change, and generate a false sense of protection from the future. In other words, by 'worrying', we set the scene to prevent changes in our lives - at least that is our hope. 'Worry', 'What if?', 'but' and 'fretting' are all symptoms of fear. We look for things to worry about, like whether it's going to rain tomorrow … or perhaps next month. A problem is something that requires a solution, but rather than seeking solutions to our current ones, we choose to find others to worry about that haven't happened yet, and may never happen. By doing this we create a great deal of stress in our bodies, often as though the hypothetical event had actually happened - muscles tighten up, we get chest pains, suffer dread, rely on old familiar comforts and make ourselves ill.

Many people don't *want* solutions to their problems, because in a perverse way their problems define who they are; paradoxically, we know what the solutions are, but prefer to ignore them by pretending that they don't exist or are unattainable. We create problems to worry about by continually putting ourselves in problematic situations; for example, like getting drunk then living in fear of being found out - perhaps by our parents or employers. However, at the same time, we're proud of and even brag about our behaviour to our peers. I remember my sister used to go to school in her uniform, but took more 'suitable' clothing with her to change into for when she truanted with her friends - worrying yet revelling in the fear of being caught. The only reason to live in fear of being found out is that we're ashamed of our own behaviour and if we're ashamed of it, why do it? We see the danger signs and walk straight past them choosing images for ourselves that make us an *acceptable* part of the 'in crowd' - it's all about peer pressure and this comes initially from films, advertising and other forms of media, like magazines.

We don't have our best interests at heart, but expect others to - how strange we are. The mind keeps us in fear of danger regardless of whether that danger exists or not and it's always on guard against attack. The ego wants to survive and is at its happiest when it's not questioned, so to speak. It's having great fun doing whatever it wants to do and when we want to stop its fun it reacts rather like a child that doesn't want to leave a playground - it has a tantrum. Worry is a way for the mind to maintain control and it's through fear-invoking control that we've been dominated for so long. When we begin to think for ourselves, the mind puts up a fight with 'worry warnings'; it creates hypothetical situations that ward off any attempt to reclaim our power. Like the mind, we want to be heard; our personal worries are greater than anyone else's; when we hear someone's story - more tragic than ours - we tend to 'tune out', waiting for a pause long enough to cut in and begin relating our own.

When we worry so much about our problems, whether hypothetical or not, we're not interested in the dilemmas of others; the ego loves to be in the limelight and it's *not* a good listener. It's a fact, that there's no-one more interested in what we have to say than ourselves.

Worry is a tool of self-confinement. For example, by worrying that we may get attacked while out shopping, we can get ourselves into such a state that we stop going out altogether - barricading ourselves into a believed place of 'safety'. I know of a lady who taped up her letterbox out of fear someone would set her house on fire during the London riots; she doesn't even live in London, but was gripped by the broadcasts and therefore, the worry. My mother didn't leave her house for years, except for hospital appointments and for Christmas dinner at my brother's house - he would pick her up and take her back again. Her only interest in the outside world came from the television which reinforced her beliefs that the outside world was unsafe - confirming that her decision not to go out of the house was the correct one, even just to sit in the garden. My mother *hated* the sun and spirituality and was never afraid to make that perfectly clear. Despite my mother never wanting to leave the house she'd still complain about the weather, even though it made no difference to her world. The more we worry about something the more extreme its effect on us. Worry is a mechanism for withdrawing from society and the outside world - it's living in a padded cell that's locked, from the inside. My mother and I were unable to converse much on the telephone because she wanted to discuss world and local scandals and to share her abhorrence of them for hours on end, but I didn't. We can never find light when we search for it in a darkened room so it's a bit of a waste of time trying, especially when someone is perfectly happy living in the dark.

'What if?' is a journey that never ends; we explore every possible negative scenario and each time we do, we increase the burden that we voluntarily carry. Worry increases our personal torment and the last thing we want to hear is that our worries are unfounded. What, after all, would we do without them? Worry is a distraction from other things we're avoiding. We use it to make excuses about why we can't help ourselves right now because if we did, the results *could* be 'catastrophic'. We create the monster we want to worry about and then flog ourselves with its whip - we flog other people with it as well, like friends or family. The monster wants to live and we continuously feed it. More than anything it wants an ally - someone to listen to its story.

Society doesn't help at all. The media provides us with a huge range of things to worry about; war, terrorism, sickness, poverty, eviction and violence are just a few examples of these. Closer to home are things like divorce, loneliness and family security; for example, we give our children mobile phones so we can remain in constant contact with them. Children are also given great worries to contend with. They're put under enormous pressure to 'perform' well in school and they're constantly pushed and examined; now they're given SATs tests at the age of seven. For what? To prove they have good memories? What exactly are we grooming them for? The parents worry and so do the children.

Later in life these children are put under greater stresses to prepare for more exams, wait months for their exam results and worry continuously about whether they've failed them. The stress is too much for some children who will always worry about 'What if I fail?' and they can spend the rest of their lives feeling inadequate if they do. I recently heard about a young boy who committed suicide because he didn't do well in his exams. A healthy society would not do this to its children and we're always too quick to blame the 'system'; *we* created this system - we *are* the system.

Worry is always negative. Who in their right mind worries about 'What if I pass my exams?' We don't worry about *success* or whether we'll enjoy the next episode of a favourite soap opera but we *do* worry about failure and how we'd fill the 'slot' if our favourite series came to an end. So what is this worry? Quite simply it's a fear of something negative; we fear it because we exclude the positives that match. For example, we talk ourselves into worrying about 'What if?' the world comes to an end but we don't want to consider 'What if it doesn't?' Worry is a low vibrational sickness of society and it's deeply embedded. We can however, choose not to live in fear and make a decision to raise our level of consciousness. This involves a decision not to submit to the will of our mind but to take back control of it; the mind, when it's in control, is negative. When I tried to talk to my mother about going out into the garden, or even walking to the gate, she became aggressive and insisted 'I can't!' But she *could* and didn't even want to try, strongly resenting any suggestion that might lead her away from her self-imprisonment. When we confine ourselves, we keep the doors closed and don't welcome any suggestion that they can be re-opened.

Just as we've locked ourselves inside our homes, we lock ourselves behind screens and through them we contact 'the world'. Even if we've been talking to someone for years online, when push comes to shove, we're mostly afraid to give out our address or phone number; our online relationships generally depend on our continued anonymity and we now have 'contacts' instead of 'friendships'. Generally speaking, we don't want to meet up with our contacts online and one of the reasons for this is that they would see us as we really are - without our masks. We worry about what's on the outside of our 'security' because we 'What if?' about someone is violent or a con-man. We worry about meeting face-to-face someone that we met *online* as we would a stranger knocking on our front door. I've known a few people to shy away when I've offered to send them a copy of my book - they didn't want to give me their address. We've been taught so well to fear strangers and people that we meet online. When we worry continuously about anything at all we're living in fear, and as long as we agree to live in fear we'll remain prisoners of our mind, and of the society we created.

~~~

Sometimes, we feel a more extreme form of fear - dread! The best way I can describe what I mean by dread is to say that it feels as though something dark and ominous has passed right through us. The emotions that go with this feeling are terror, apprehension and an overwhelming feeling of imminent danger. We learn early on to be afraid, from listening to various types of bedtime stories such as *Peter Pan*, *The Three Little Pigs* or perhaps *Jack and the Beanstalk*. They're hardly friendly foundations for young, innocent and highly impressionable children. Some of us also picked up these fears from our parents or guardians and some are inherited from other sources. We learnt to be afraid of pirates, giants, tyrants, ogres, burglars under the bed and bogeymen - the list goes on and on. Thought is memory; if you can think it, it's from memory. We've built up all these memories of fears and added to them from sources such as films and other media. More than the memories themselves we remember the emotions related to them - the actual feeling of fear - and it's important to note here that our fears are nothing more than thoughts. We've all learnt something about history and what stands out more than anything, is that we've always been at war and that war is brutal and heartless. Our minds are awash with horrific images so it's no wonder we know so well how to feel afraid. There's no greater fear than dread so what can we do about it. When it happens, just allow it to pass through - be aware of it and don't resist; it can't harm you in any way. As you become more aware it will occur less frequently and less intensely. This process is faster if we don't subject ourselves to further conditioning from violent films, newscasts or other media terrors. We can choose to watch it all and suffer further, or to focus on our awareness and the beauty of the Now. Here are a few more 'What if?' scenarios for you to ponder over:

- What if you're truly amazing?
- What if we're missing the point?
- What if we're here to experience?
- What if we stopped fighting?
- What if there's no such thing as death?
- What if our purpose is to raise our consciousness level?

Imagine dying and then being offered the opportunity to return for a week. The world would be exactly as it is right now, but you couldn't be harmed in any way. What would you choose to do with that week that you haven't done before? I've asked a few friends this and not one could come up with an answer.

You're everything! You're a conduit through which the divine speaks and there's no 'What if?' about it. No-one can see through your eyes - your perspective belongs to you alone. We know so much more than we've been led to believe and deep down we've no doubts - no academic institution can teach us this. Our energy has been suppressed and *misused*, but I can assure you it's still there and no-one can take it away from us, come what may. It's not born and it doesn't die. The only reasons we can't feel it is because we haven't been encouraged to ask relevant questions about our lives, and our focus has been directed towards the transient rather than the infinite - it's based on desire. We listen with our ears and see with our eyes but these are so limited in Universal terms; more important than what we see and hear, are what we *don't* and this information is available to anyone - no exclusions and no prejudices. Consciousness can be perceived only through the heart. You're the world … Now … not in the future.

Emotions and Energy

Emotions are a highly volatile energetic state.

Our emotions are one of the most powerful energetic forces that we know of. Unchecked, mishandled or manipulated, negative emotions can cause enormous harm to ourselves and those around us - the reverberations of which can be felt for many years to come. Conversely, positive emotions can be a force for much good - no-one ever went to war because they were joyful and happy. How we greet each day and move through it depends on our emotions, but not only that, other people's emotions can have an effect on us too. It isn't until we *sit down quietly* and think about this, that the connection between emotions and energy become apparent.

We've all experienced walking down the road and felt the mood of other people as they approach us. Often we sense if they're angry, afraid, depressed, happy, sad, guilty, ashamed or hostile. What we're actually picking up on is their energy (emotional state) and we adjust our actions accordingly; for example, if we perceive that an approaching group of people is hostile we may choose to cross the road, thus avoiding potential conflict. There are many ways in which we read people's body language; we know when they look downcast, suspicious or walk with confidence. Their emotions might have come from pent up feelings from many years ago or an event they experienced just moments earlier, like meeting up with an old friend. We read each other all the time without realising that we're doing it and have no idea how we pick up this energetic information; the process is automatic and acts rather like an early warning system enabling us to react appropriately; this is how we read our world.

Most of us have felt the energy in a room when we unsuspectingly walk in on an argument, or the tension between two people who aren't speaking to each other. Perhaps you've been present when an employee is being humiliated by their boss? I'm sure we can all relate to one of these 'cut the atmosphere with a knife' situations. In most cases differences aren't put aside when we arrive because the need to continue with being *right* is greater than any need to be polite for the sake of someone else - neither party will give in even for a moment. The energy is bouncing around and because it's low vibration we feel tense, awkward and 'dragged down' with an urgent need to leave the room as soon as possible. These situations are difficult enough to cope with, but they exist in the 'physical world' and at least we can be sure of the mood and personality of the company we're in. However, the internet has removed vital parts of our 'communication skills' and now we can't rely on gestures or other physical cues like intonation or eye-contact. We act purely on the words, images and emoticons we see on the screen, which can so easily be - and often are - misconstrued.

In this world of the web, we transmit and receive energetic information - instantly - when communicating with each other. This makes it hard to accurately judge what the person we're talking to is *really* feeling, or what their true intentions are; feelings can't be replaced or translated by crude digital expressions of our faces. We can't hide our feelings when we're standing face-to-face, but online we've the option of telling a different story. For example the acronym for 'rolling on the floor laughing' - 'rofl'. Often this is not what we're feeling at all, and we know no-one actually does it. Depending on the conversation we could be crying and at the same time typing 'rofl' in order to hide our emotions; for example, hurt feelings. 'Rofl' can be a mask to cover our emotions or intentions; we portray ourselves as invulnerable. We can hide our intentions when we talk face-to-face as well, but this is much harder to do and sometimes our true feelings stand out a mile. Imagine a face-to-face conversation where you take the time to choose which facial expression you're going to display.

This idea is ridiculous, but this is *exactly* what we do online and it can get awkward if we accidentally click on the wrong emoticon and press send - we can't do that when we're talking face-to-face but we *can* get away with it online. We live in a world of choreographed feelings and emotions manifested as emoticons. The emoticons are a representation of our 'virtual persona' and more often than not, this is vastly different from the physical one - it's just another mask.

Politicians and actors (amongst others) are trained in all aspects of body language so that they know how to stand, smile, position their hands and how to make eye-contact for best effect. There's a great deal more to this language and we're pretty expert at it - even without training. In the case of politicians, they learn it in order to convince the public to believe in them and feign personal strength and ability. The fact that they have to *learn* it means they don't have the right character for the job, which is why they need a fake persona. If we need to be taught how to be convincing, then we don't believe in what we're saying and for the well-trained eye, the deception is obvious. Humanity is genius when it comes to creating characters, which is how we can become such good actors and create things like caricatures or puppets so well. In order to become a good actor or politician we have to be able to hide our true self and in particular, our true emotions. Body language is a tool that can make or break a politician, actor or perhaps a salesman; if their energy isn't tuned in correctly, we're unconvinced by them.

~~~

If we look at online videos that allow comments we often see capitalisation (SHOUTING), which makes these remarks antagonistic and therefore awaiting a response from anyone who'll pick up on the energy - it's a trap. Shouting is an emotional outburst that states what we're saying doesn't hold enough weight on its own, which is why it needs to be reinforced. It also tells the reader, quite clearly, that whoever is shouting isn't going to listen to anyone's responses. If the comments don't get responded to, they end right there, but if we reply to the comment then a string of further and more heated abuse follows - just about everyone is aware of how nasty these threads can become. Whoever wrote the comment loves the reactions that help him to express himself to the rest of humanity, in the way that he chooses - he feeds off their energy. Those who continuously respond, also like the way the aggressor's hostile comments make them feel. The aggressors love the power it gives them, because they can't experience it in their *real* life; likewise, others must enjoy being caught in their net. I doubt anyone has ever given someone a 'telling off' online and successfully changed their attitude - quite the contrary. These threads act as magnets for those looking to vent their spleen on the world; whoever is shouting on these threads is really expressing his pent up feelings and the louder he shouts, the more emotional he becomes, and the more energy he leaves on the threads to be picked up by other viewers, should they choose to pick it up. These threads are powerful emotional outlets and people feel safe venting on them. More often than not a thread is attacked because something in it resonated with the aggressor - he doesn't feel good and neither do the respondents - sometimes it's due to pure mischief.

This pattern is similar to our relationship with governments or other authorities; they call the shots and we respond, but we don't change them when we're silent and they're not listening well enough to the few who do speak out. If we choose to walk away (say 'No'), then they have no power, for their power comes from our willingness to respond to them. Next time you walk past a newsagent look at the headlines in the papers - they're capitalised and bold (both are shouting). This powerful energy affects us and our response is as negative as the headline intended it to be - our emotions have been hijacked and someone else is in control of how we feel. When we realise this we're able to take back control of our emotions and the headlines lose their power over us - we don't pick up the energy they emit. What's happening between us all is an energetic exchange; if we don't control our own power, someone else will.

Emotion = e-motion = energy in motion

People who pick up on this energy can still feel it even months or years after it was written. The same applies to re-reading a much-treasured stack of love letters or a sad film we watch again and again. We feel and react with the same emotions as if we're seeing them for the first time - whoever sees them - in varying degrees - feels the emotion. Energy flows out of us, and it flows back in. We're constantly sending out and absorbing energy to and from a variety of sources and it's important to become aware of this. We may leave our house one morning feeling buoyant, in which case this is the energy we're emitting; however, seeing sensational headlines or meeting a friend who's always full of 'doom and gloom' can drain that energy and suddenly, that buoyant feeling evaporates and is replaced with a feeling of imminent doom.

~~~

I'd like to share with you something that happened to me not so long ago when I lived in France. I was driving with my partner to a builder's merchant. A police car appeared behind me and flagged us over. When we stopped, two policemen got out. One of them looked friendly enough, but the other had an aggressive strut and was clearly 'on a mission'. Even though it wasn't sunny, he was wearing sunglasses. I smiled, but it was not returned. I asked the officer why I'd been stopped and he said that I'd been talking on a mobile phone whilst I was driving and he looked really pleased that he'd caught me. From that point on he couldn't express the energy he wanted to because I got out, offered him my handbag and gestured that he could search it and my car too. I informed him that he was mistaken, because neither I nor my partner had a mobile phone with us. He insisted that we did, and his partner smiled, knowing full well that his colleague was stuck in a hole of his own digging. He never admitted his error or apologised and went off frustrated. This unexpressed energy is always re-absorbed and will probably get expressed all the stronger on the next person he pulls over, or perhaps in some other situation. All our pent up emotions must get expressed and vented sooner or later.

Think of a kettle about to boil. The gas or electricity is the life force, and the water our emotions. If we block the vent that allows the steam to escape then pressure builds up inside. Sooner or later the kettle will explode and then there'll be a sudden outburst of steam (emotion). When we 'let off steam' in this way, it hurts us, and anyone unfortunate enough to be caught in the blast. However, when we allow the steam to escape freely no harm is done and the system works harmoniously. Allowing emotions to control us prevents us from being grounded - we're always reacting and rarely in a calm state. It's unwise to allow ourselves to be led by our emotions - they're highly unstable.

Moods are also emotions and they can last for weeks or years. We often don't know why we're in a particular mood, because we can't remember when we started feeling it. However, moods come from suppressed emotions and manifest themselves in things like irritation or anger. We've all met people who are always irritated or angry. My entire teens and twenties were spent in these moods but occasionally I could vent, often by grabbing something and hurling it across the room; I wasn't too selective about what or where I threw objects either. Once when I threw a brick, I missed a man's head by an inch. When pent up emotions erupt, we don't think about what we're going to break or the consequences - rational thought ceases. This is because the need to get these pent up feelings out of our system is far greater than the value of any object we might break in the process. We don't think in these situations - we're in the Now. Sometimes we feel much better after our outburst and sometimes the effects aren't so visible, but they're still there. When we become aware of what's actually going on we're able to regain control of our lives, if we want to.

~~~

Energy is a collective and powerful experience when we're gathered in groups. The energy bounces between us and multiplies - like at music festivals. Freddie Mercury for example, could really stir up an audience - the bigger the crowd the more powerful the energy. Supporters at a football match emit an enormous amount of energy because of their sheer numbers. Have you ever heard one end of a stadium when a goal is scored? The energy from the crowd can spur on a team to perform well. If the supporters of *Team A* are more encouraging and active than the supporters in *Team B* the chances are *Team A* will win the match - they're spurred on because of the energy emitted by the crowd. We can feel this energy even if we're not there, by watching it on the television for example. Those who gather en masse in a pub to watch a match also feel the energy and consequently, roar out with their own. Similarly, a person sitting at home alone watching a match (I know one of these) will lift off his seat when his team scores a goal - distance is no object for this energy.

Emotions need to be expressed and we'd struggle to interact without them. How could we understand each other if we didn't cry, laugh, sulk, shout or get angry for example? These are our ways of relating to each other and also to ourselves. Like with the steam in the kettle, our emotions need to escape from inside us. Because emotions are energy and we pick up on them, some amusing situations can occur. If for example a person is laughing uncontrollably, it's almost impossible not to join in, even if we don't know what they're laughing at - it's infectious and can result in a painful stitch; this type of laughter is physically exhausting. Similarly, we can pick up on energy from yawning or crying by another person and involuntarily do the same - mirroring their emotions.

Emotions are an energetic way of expressing what we're feeling at the time. Too often, we don't recognise why we're feeling them at all - the cause can go back many years. Way into my thirties I'd react to events in much the same way as I did in my childhood. If I saw events on television that were similar to things that happened to me, I'd feel the same emotions, such as sadness, fear, dread and frustration; what I saw acted as a trigger to re-awaken older memories - it was as though I were re-living the experience through somebody else. Unlike online with emoticons, these emotions aren't always controllable - particularly when what caused them is deep-seated. How we cope with emotion is different for everybody. Some people can cry over minor events, and others can't cry at all. These emotions, however, belong to all of us and like with my example of a kettle, too often we suppress them.

Peace of mind can *only* be found within; the process is hard work and a full-time job on top of whatever else we have to do. However, the more we get to grips with being honest about our own behaviour and character, the more peaceful we become inside. By becoming aware of our own energy, in for example, conversations with other people, we become self-regulating and consequently, our world becomes a calmer place to live in. But, if we speak aggressively and constantly complain about other people we're putting out a lot of negativity, which comes back and adds to the burden we already carry - we become negativity generators. Another way to look at this is to ask 'If you met yourself, would you want to be your own friend?' or when you're talking to someone, online or off, ask yourself whether you'd like to receive the energy you're emitting. It doesn't matter if we slip up every now and then, what matters is persevering, getting to really know ourselves, and with practice we'll slip less and less. A most important point about energy is to avoid or say goodbye to those who continually want to drain ours. Because we pick up on energy it's not a good idea to remain in the company of those who want to pass theirs onto us - unless it's good energy. Our own energy is precious, and when we become aware of the significance of that knowledge, we're no longer willing to part with it, or to take on the negative energy of others - it's not even an option.

Observation

To observe effectively we need to zoom out - not in.

When we think about observation it tends to fall into one of three categories: something we do, like looking through a telescope, something we have, like the ability to be observant and something we're under, like the ubiquitous security camera. When I first heard the term 'observation' with regard to my thoughts and looking for truth within, I couldn't for the life of me see how that was possible. All I could think of was that my veins, lungs, kidneys and other internal bodily parts are just that - on the inside - and my eyes look outwards. There was also a bigger problem - I'd no idea what I was supposed to be observing or what this so-called 'Now' was all about. Before even *starting* this 'observation', my mind stuck out its big foot and tripped me up - I hadn't reached the first hurdle and was already flat on my face. I'd barely picked myself up when my mind pushed me back down again. It told me I wasn't qualified to do the job and that I'm not an 'expert'. Can anyone be more of an expert on who I really am than *me*? We're generally conditioned to believe that we need professional help for such matters - we most certainly don't for this. Experience is a good teacher but it's no substitute for observation and no-one else can observe for us. It doesn't matter how good the teacher is if the student is inattentive or unwilling to learn. When we observe our mad world it becomes clear that we're all students, no matter what our age, who still have much to learn. No one person can observe or change the chaos of the world, but we can, without a shadow of a doubt, change ourselves and only this will produce the results that most people refuse to give credence to.

Observing ourselves can be tough because our mind interferes all the time - it's insistent and keeps us blinkered within a limited physical perspective, and doesn't have any spare time for airy-fairy will-o'-the-wisp metaphysical nonsense. It wants information, hard evidence, debate, paperwork, action, analysis, cross-referencing and above all, it wants to maintain control - it doesn't want our interference. When considering a project for example, the mind reminds us of our previous failures and tells us there's not much point in wasting our precious time, as based on past evidence, the project is *doomed*. The mind wants to keep us in our place - it doesn't want to change and it doesn't want a 'co-director'. When we decide to observe our thoughts the mind interrupts and before we know it, often before we've even begun, we check for email messages, phone a friend, make a drink, water the garden, awaken an ancient grudge or clean out a kitchen cupboard. We may find that we're staring at a blank wall, a crack on the ceiling and eerily, sometimes we're staring at nothing at all, dreamily unaware of our thoughts - in the latter case we're 'out of mind'. The mind knows a lot of pressing postponement techniques to occupy us with, should we become distracted from what it thinks we should be doing. More often than not it bombards us with thoughts that keep us in 'take no action' mode. On the whole we're unaware of the process but it's possible, if we pay attention, to observe the insane stream of unimportant data coming and going.

The mind does all this so fast that, by the time we've finished our chores, we've quite forgotten what it was we wanted to consider; the thought has been dispersed and replaced by a multitude of other 'high priority' tasks that are more to the mind's liking. Whenever we want freedom from the chatter of our mind it presents us with meaningless hypnotic distractions. It's only a matter of time before questions like 'Who Am I?' for example, shout out our name again and the cycle recommences.

~~~

There's something that drives us to question the meaning of our existence, at some point in our lives.

It's always there at the back of our minds, but we tend to ignore it in favour of more 'important' pastimes. Initially, the concepts are unfathomable, as our minds have been trained to be rigid and negative. Generally, the only acceptable knowledge is from our education and various other equally ritualised conditioning processes. Searching for alternative information in books and on the internet about the mystery schools, hidden secrets or this thing called 'enlightenment' is like wallpapering over the existing paper in a room - the lumps and bumps will show through. We have to *first* strip off the old embedded ideas, prejudices and beliefs etc. There are so many layers to get through and lots of elbow grease is needed. This metaphorical room is our responsibility alone, and no-one can do the work for us - it's unpaid and arduous. The room is a part of each and every one of us and it's 'Private Property'; we own it outright and always will. It's our 'observatory' and we've let it get into a dreadful mess - sooner or later, we need to clear it out. At this point, I'd like to mention that we don't need books or the internet in order to enquire about our true nature; this knowledge is accessible to everyone on the planet and with observation, if we truly want to, we'll find what we're looking for. So never give up because you already know all of this - you're remembering it. Don't trust in the mind that will tell you there's 'no proof' and that you're 'wasting your time', because everybody needs to see and think about this too, if it's going to have any impact on society; don't trust in *anything* other than your own rational voice. *You* are your world and only *you* can change it.

Initially, when we observe ourselves; for example, by challenging the mind, things seem rather strange. Imagine you're driving along a motorway and you're almost out of petrol. You're about to pass a service station and the sign tells you there's another station in forty miles. The mind tells us we'll make it to the second station but the other voice in our heads says 'be wise and fill up here'. However, we tend to listen to the mind, as this is our familiar habit, but, this habit gets us into familiar situations - the mind lives on the edge of danger. If we're serious about observing and changing our destructive habits, we'll begin to listen to the more rational voice. When we challenge the negativity of our mind we're moving 'mountains' and the more we do it, the more it becomes second nature, as it were. The first step is to accept that we have destructive habits and the second, to decide that we're through with suffering; yes, it's a decision we have to make. When we make a decision to listen to the rational voice something in us changes; the more we listen to it, the more we change and the less we pollute our world with negative energy and thought; we no longer allow the insane mind to control our thoughts - we break the pattern and change direction. In other words, we become responsible for our thoughts and choose which to listen to. When we change direction a great deal about human behaviour becomes clear.

Let's take the newspapers and television broadcasts for example, and think about why we pay so much attention to them. We never get good news except maybe when someone has grown a giant pumpkin exceeding any previously seen at garden shows, or a politician kisses a baby on the cheek - other than that we may get the occasional good news, but it's not *our* good news and it doesn't benefit humanity in any way. Some people say they *have* to keep up with the news, but these papers get read, the stories get spread in concentrated horror via other media (we call it *social*) and then, before we've fully digested yesterday's bad news, another helping is offered up to tempt our hungry minds. Absorbing this bad news every day is never beneficial - it's nothing more than regularly feeding on 'anxiety and depression' flavoured snacks. Consumed daily, this 'food' becomes bland, and no longer startles us - even though we proclaim 'horror'. If we don't read the news, people think we don't care or that we're closing our eyes to *reality* and if we do then at best we can only join in the spreading of bad news; we can't, practically, do anything about any of it. This doesn't make sense to me at all and if that's 'reality' why do we want to hold onto it so badly? When we pull away from the *River of Disaster* - in which all things flow - we observe it from a distance and therefore, from a wider perspective. We observe that humanity, on the whole, really doesn't want to change the world it's living in - otherwise, why is there so much resistance to dispense with the things that drag us down so much? Removing this negative force from our lives has many benefits on our health and mental well-being - life slows down and with it the chaos in our mind.

As ideas and realisations fall into unfamiliar places, and things we once thought were solid, like our world, aren't any more, all lies get revealed; the hardest lies of all to accept are those we've been telling ourselves for so long - yes, we all tell them at some point in our lives. One of the reasons this is hard to cope with is that in the past, we've projected our abhorrence of lies onto others and now we realise that *we* do it too. Applying the social labels 'liar' or 'hypocrite' to ourselves is a hard-hitting experience - like catching sight of ourselves in a mirror and being appalled by our own reflection. It quickly becomes apparent that we're no better than anyone else in this world - a humbling and surprisingly liberating experience.

At this point we've two choices - ignore what we've seen, as we've done for many years, or continue to observe these ever-evolving revelations. Each time we recognise a shortcoming in ourselves is like stripping off one of our masks; these have become so adhered to our faces that we don't realise we're wearing them. On a deeper level of this observation is the revelation that what we've criticised in others was a projection from deep within ourselves. We're so deeply conditioned against being duped by scams, con-artists or dodgy-builders for example, that we don't recognise we're conning ourselves.

The biggest lie that permeates society is that our life is an accident of nature, and that there's nothing after it. We one hundred percent physicalise our existence and kid ourselves that there's nothing after our deaths. But this is a cop out - it's an excuse to justify our temporary enjoyment of the pleasures we cherish so much. We justify this enjoyment in order that we don't have to make an effort to change our habitual behaviour; for example, abstaining from wild parties, playing non-stop games or drinking alcohol and eating to excess - anyone who tries to tell us otherwise is labelled a 'party pooper'. We're just a bit too quick to stick critical labels on anyone who disagrees with our conditioned beliefs, even though we don't believe them ourselves. However, these things make our lives more bearable because we forget or at least ignore our problems, albeit temporarily. The mind is more than able to continue this unproductive cycle and plays 'devil's advocate' when it comes to the welfare of humanity. It does this by ignoring our connection to consciousness and putting our thoughts and insights down to something physical; in other words, it makes consciousness, or Spirit, into something 'biodegradable' and therefore 'disposable'. We trample down our conscience, always looking to people who'll provide *proofs* to confirm what we want to believe. When we hear what we don't want to hear (like perhaps from this book) although we can see it makes sense, we convince ourselves that it doesn't. We excuse ourselves and seek new reasons not to think on what our lives are really about.

We can observe our behaviour in many situations and this is necessary, if we want to end our suffering. One way to do this is to watch our reactions to others; for example, by comparing what we're thinking when we talk to them, with what we're actually saying - more often than not they don't match. We can also compare what we really think about someone when we tell them they 'look good', when we don't mean it. By observing in these ways we begin to realise that we're far from honest and then as that realisation sinks in and becomes palatable, we change our behaviour accordingly. My life changed for the better when I took responsibility for my thoughts and how I felt about other people changed too. Without being prepared to go through a process of self-observation this wouldn't have been possible. When we make an excuse about why we can't do something or change an obsessive habit we're in fact, confirming our will to remain just as we are. All these things are observable and tell us a great deal about ourselves, if we're prepared to examine them honestly and closely enough. Mostly we're not prepared to be honest about our own behaviour because, let's face it, we're all headstrong and determined to do what we want, regardless of whether it's in our best interest or not; none of us like being judged by anyone else - let alone by *ourselves*. Even if we ask the advice of others, we generally have no intention of listening to it. Paramount to self-reflection is a willingness to criticise our own motives, actions and intentions, rather than those of others. This book and everything in it are me doing the same - how can it be anything else? The book came into being because I made an active decision to follow the 'white rabbit'; I've no choice but to continue following it and this is where it has led me, so far.

By stripping off our masks, usually one at a time, we make ourselves vulnerable to outside criticism - something nobody really enjoys. Ironically, when this happens we no longer care what anyone thinks *or* need their approval. This process can take time but I assure you it's worth the effort; when we dispense with the need for masks, barriers or approval we find that our fears subside. We wear so many of these masks and only realise we're wearing them after self-reflecting, *without* allowing our pride or ego to interfere. There are many ways to know ourselves and once we start enquiring one thing leads to another - it's a continuous process. The masks represent a sort of defence system; they act as a shield to hide anything that might render us vulnerable to attack. Have you ever noticed your thoughts during an argument or how you try to stop yourself revealing your true feelings to the person you're arguing with? Have you noticed your thoughts when arguing and know you're being obstinate, but won't admit to it? Try to catch your thoughts during these moments and recognise how ingenious we are when it comes to defending 'our corner' regardless of rights or wrongs; I've done quite a lot of this in my time, and now, each time I end up laughing at the genius of it all. Try also to notice your thoughts when you're going to sleep. At first when I did this I always fell asleep before I got the chance to notice patterns but now, after persevering, I watch my own 'demons' coming and going and find it rather fun to do. Catch yourself out at the supermarket when you're paying for shopping; watch the thoughts about the cashier or the people in front of or behind you. I used to find some people rather intimidating and others I felt I had power over. What are you thinking now, about me or yourself, after reading this paragraph? Perhaps you're judging me and that's okay, but more important than judging me is to recognise and accept that you're doing it, rather than getting caught up in the critical net. The point of observation is not to watch me, but to watch *you* - this is the tricky part. The more we observe, the more we see and the more we change - provided we resist the urge to be 'hurt' or 'offended'. Through this type of observation it becomes obvious that there's an observer that's neither the ego nor the mind.

The ego dominates and is defended by the mind that created it. As long as we believe that we're the ego, we're unable to observe ourselves and the reason for this is that we filter out the *Observer*. By this subterfuge we've become accustomed to seeing the world through *conditioned* eyes as others would have us see it, rather than as it is. This predicament leaves us psychologically ill-equipped to *observe* the world we've created, so that close examination of something 'magnificent' - like a flower, or the gathering of its pollen by a bee - becomes just a scientific and logical exercise, as opposed to something *miraculous* - the mind filters out true beauty. Close observation of our mind is impossible without the awareness of our two contradictory voices. Once we become aware of their differences it becomes difficult, if not impossible, to ignore the voice that's in our highest interest.

Attachment

*We place a noose around our necks and
tell ourselves it'll keep us from falling.*

At its simplest level, attachment is anything or anyone that we allow to control our thoughts and actions, in any given situation. A dog's movements are restricted when he's attached to a lead, and a train carriage coupled to its engine isn't going anywhere, unless it's being pulled. The dog goes where its owner wants it to, and the carriage as far along the track as the engine pulls it. In these examples, attachment enables *control* and it's a good thing that it does - who knows what the dog may get up to if he were let loose, or what damage would result from a carriage that became uncoupled from its engine. There are many ways in which attachment is vital; for example, mountain climbers rely on being attached to their rope, power cables to their poles and our arms and legs to our bodies - to say nothing of our heads! There are also many ways in which attachment is a detriment to our lives; for example, when we live in fear of losing our home, job or partner - when the very thought of losing them leaves us feeling insecure.

At this point, I find myself wondering which attachment has the greatest power over humanity - money or people. In my experience, my family were largely controlled by their love of money and material things -

what these did for their image and bank accounts meant far more to them than any person ever could. My sister and I were placed in an orphanage so that my father could work and play freely, without the responsibility of small children around. It's funny how we become so attached to the things that we can never keep; people love accumulating money as much as they love beating a high score in a game - there's something about having more and more that runs through our veins - whether it be pounds, points, food or online followers. Given a choice, there are many that would give up their children or partner, rather than their home or belongings; if we're honest with ourselves, we love things far more than we do people, even our own children. It becomes a question of priority.

Imagine you're in a relationship, and you've managed to scrape together enough money to buy your own home - albeit with a hefty mortgage. After a year or two of bliss, things begin to turn sour and you separate. What then becomes more important - salvaging as much as you can from your investment, or the loss of your partner? I've had much experience of these situations both of my own, and of other people who I've known; in every case money and belongings were the highest priority, for at least one of the parties involved. Over time, we become attached to the things we call 'ours' and I'd suggest this is not a good thing. For one thing, they prevent us from having honest and open relationships, because those belongings get in the way of them; take for example, so-called prenuptial agreements - a sort of 'I love you, but, should we split up I want to leave with everything that was mine before we got into this relationship, intact'; this sort of relationship is hardly based on love. Even if there's not an agreement, we still tend to want what was ours to begin with - of course there are exceptions, but I doubt there are many of them.

Money aside, we can become so attached to people that we get ourselves into a situation in which we believe we can't live without them. I've done this many times and as a result gone from one relationship to another, because I feared being alone again. When a relationship ends, for whatever reason, it takes us out of our comfort zone and we have to rebuild our lives, routines and rituals all over again - from scratch. Even the thought of such disruption can be too much to cope with; so much so, that many people stay in unhealthy relationships because they don't want to experience the upheaval of starting all over again, or living alone. I got to the point where I'd hear myself saying 'oh well, here I go again' and somehow, always landed back on my feet - stronger after each experience. The attachment here is to a *relationship*, rather than the person - an attachment to someone, *anyone,* to share the burden of this life with; let's face it, life, in our society, isn't exactly a 'picnic'.

Attachment to friends and family can be similarly burdensome; things run smoothly until, as we've probably all experienced, they don't. People have different ideas about what they expect from each other and the problem here is that rarely are two people's thoughts in line. As an example, let's take a family whose children have left home; the parents then decide to split up and go their separate ways, and the children are less than happy about it - this scenario is not uncommon. Children expect their parents to remain together and keep the home fires burning, as it were, even though they no longer have a need for it. When I was living on the River Thames my children rarely came to visit me, and then only at my request; when I told them I was going to move to France they weren't particularly happy about it and at the time, I was rather surprised by this; however, they didn't need me around, so I went anyway; had things been different I would perhaps have stayed in England. Sometimes we *have* to let go of the things holding us in place - the things to which we've granted control of our lives - sentimentality especially, can stop us from realising our dreams or expanding on our visions. We get one chance to do the things we want to do in this life and, provided we don't shed our responsibilities, we should go out and do them.

As mentioned earlier, attachment enables control and this is not always a good thing - least of all when we're on a conscientious spiritual 'journey'. Many years ago I was attached to a particular vegetarian snack from a local store. I ate them for years and then one day couldn't find them; the store had decided not to stock them anymore, which left me at a bit of a loss as to what to replace them with. I'd become dependent on that store for the supply, assuming quite wrongly that this product would always be available. After that I developed a recipe for my own similar alternative snacks, which tasted better. When we're attached to something, it has control over us and there's a risk of losing it - we also stifle our own creativity. For example, when we follow -

to the letter - a recipe, we forget that we can adapt them for ourselves. Anything we're attached to controls us; even the simple things, like a chair, mug or book: we can for example, become upset if someone sits in our favourite chair, drinks from our mug or dog-ears one of our books; interference with the things we're attached to bring out our negative feelings and emotions - they have control over us. Remember, the engine pull's the carriage, the owner controls the dog.

I've a friend who keeps all her clothes. She's in her mid-fifties and still has some of her clothes from when she was fifteen. How she finds the room to store them all is beyond me, but her double fitted wardrobes are packed from top to bottom including the one in her spare room. Depending on the season, these clothes get moved into and out of her attic. When I asked why she does this her reply was 'I don't like waste'. Surely it's more of a waste to cram them into cupboards and not use them. Anyway, I don't believe this excuse and I'd suggest, it's more about a fear of loss or going without one day. It's also about attachment to the memories of when she wore them and her lost youth. She won't like me writing about her *lost youth*, but then I'll remind her of a request for me to make her younger than her *mid-fifties*.

Just as we hold onto belongings, we hold onto memories of them - in photograph frames or diaries. For example, I remember many years ago being unable to delete a friend's phone number from my address book - he'd died six months earlier. For the first few months I used to dial the number hoping he'd answer. Realising that we must let go is difficult, but we all have to do it sooner or later. I couldn't comprehend how someone could leave and never come back. Humanity coming together only to suffer and then separate again made no sense to me then, and it still doesn't. We shed tears year after year for the same pains - digging up past memories and reliving the misery of them again and again. The tears we shed expressed our loss years ago, but they won't help now. Sorrow is difficult to live with - it's devastating and can take a long time to recover from. There's no need to forget our friends who die, but it's possible to re-frame how we look at death - we all die sooner or later. We have to stop looking at death as though it were unnatural - it's as natural as our births. Yes, we can die from terrible illnesses, but death itself is *not* an illness and there's no need to treat it as such. Death from illness is simply death brought about sooner than we would die naturally. Illness is a dreadful thing but if we look at it objectively then surely it would be prudent to ask 'Why is there so much illness in this world?', which we can do something about, rather than 'Why is there so much death?', which we can't.

Observing our actions enables us to question them. For example, we can examine whether a process we hold onto is good for us, by asking:

- Is this in my highest interest?
- Have I reached my fullest potential?
- Am I doing myself more harm than good?
- Do I want these nightmares to end?

When we ask the above questions the honest answer can only be 'Yes' or 'No'. However, too often we reply

'Yes, but' or 'No, but'. 'But', in this sense, is a weasel word - an escape route that *qualifies* our answer. It's a limitation we place on ourselves and it's nothing more than resistance to letting go of our self-directed dramas. We can, if we choose to, resist that resistance. 'But' is attachment; 'yes' and 'but' can't exist harmoniously together and neither can 'no' and 'but'. 'But' is the excuse we use to disagree with the 'yes' or 'no'. 'But' is a clause, a condition and a doubt. 'yes, but' or 'no, but' are formulas that can't be solved. 'But' is a self-imposed mitigation. 'But' is the small print; it's our terms and conditions before signing.

The greatest attachment of all is to our ego. The ego is born from the mind - it's a manifestation of it - the mind also creates our 'virtual' ego. The mind wants to hold on to its control and we don't particularly care who's in charge - as long as it's not us. We've absorbed our environment through religion, society, family, culture and education - now we project selective parts of it as our *self* - our ego.

Ego = Energy Going Out.

What we project and put on display as 'who we are' is our ego, but it's not who we truly are. Ego is the force that hides our true nature - it's our disguise and the image of ourselves that we project onto others. Whatever we project produces a reaction in our own lives; for one thing, we have to keep up the façade, which means we have to hide behind our masks. We're multi-faceted, not just a body, and we don't realise it. We cling onto the ego, feeding it when it so desires, and it's not until we recognise it for what it is - a faux entity - that we're able to shed our masks, at which point the world becomes a very different place to live in.

Have you ever had a bad argument with someone and been really angry with them? We say things we don't mean and then feel shame and guilt when we reflect on it later on. On another level, we know that the hurtful things we said came from our 'shadow' and it *does* mean them. We want to stop ourselves but we're unable to. Our reactions to events are protective of any part of us that'll be left vulnerable when we're 'under attack'.

It's only by reflecting on our character and observing how we react in certain situations that we become aware of our separation from the rest of the world. Separation leads us to believe that we're better or worse than everyone else. We place a barrier between the two and keep it tightly closed, allowing no trespassers. It's only in anger or other highly emotional moments that our shadow bursts forth, sometimes with devastating effects; for example, when our backs are up against a wall. Why do we need it? It's a part of us and without it we're incomplete. By locking our shadow away we're unable to cope with everything put in front of us. We need to deflate the ego and embrace our shadow, so that they become one. When they do there's no need to wear masks - thus enabling us to relax our grip and let go of the fear that our 'dark side' might be exposed. Though our shadow has the capacity to embrace 'hell' itself, it doesn't mean we have to go there. The shadow isn't all dark however; there is much we hide that is *good* too; such as, talents we don't have the confidence to develop, or healthy emotions that we fear to express; when we hide something, it's because we don't want anyone else to find it. When our shadow and ego become one, we're no longer afraid of 'vulnerability' and we no longer feel threatened by society - we then appear to the outside world as we really are and more importantly, we appear to *ourselves* as we really are.

Attachments keep us living in the past; perhaps in a constant state of sorrow because someone we loved died, or a state of mistrust, hatred or anger caused by some other experience. These attachments can literally make us physically and psychologically ill. As I've discussed before, our minds are inclined toward the negative and therefore, the things that upset us in the past are the things that play on our minds now. We can all remember events that brought joy into our lives, even momentarily; for example, when we received a gift, or on our wedding day, or a chance meeting, but they rarely occupy our minds except for the odd sentimental moments as we glance at a picture on a shelf, or the gift we were once given. When we become aware of our daily thoughts and activities we gain a greater understanding of the things that make us 'tick' - with that understanding, we take back control of our lives; we can't control society as a whole, but we can control how we interact within it.

Letting go of our attachments doesn't mean letting go of all people and things; it means not allowing them to control what you do, think or feel - it makes you master of yourself. There are those who won't be happy about that, but then they're free to let go of *you*, should they wish to, and they invariably do; *if* they do, then they weren't a positive force in your life to begin with. As we let go of attachments our awareness is bound to change; the things we once thought of as precious become meaningless, and the people we once thought of as friends can become more distant, unless they grow with you. To grow in awareness does require a certain amount of sacrifice - obviously; we can't change *and* at the same time, remain the same. We must first strip ourselves of *everything* - then and only then can we don new clothes.

Once we realise just how much control attachments have over our lives and make the decision to take it back, where do we start? That's a good question, and it's likely that a 'one-size-fits-all' answer is impossible. I can tell you how I did it, which might give you pointers in helping you make a start. To begin with, I had lots of DVDs and books that I was never going to watch or read again and decided to take them to a charity shop, which I did, albeit bit by bit. There were some that I put back on the shelf 'just in case', but it wasn't long before I got rid of those as well. I came to love the empty spaces on my shelves, and the fact that when I bought a new DVD I didn't have to find a space to cram it into. I then turned my attention to my clothes and shoes and anything that I hadn't worn for the last five years, sentiment aside, followed the trail of the DVDs and books.

I started small, tackled the easier things first and then moved onto the larger and more difficult ones - only we, as individuals, know what they are. When past memories torment me, as they still do at times, I look directly at them, ask where they came from and what they're doing in my mind right now. I tell myself that I am 'here', 'now', and that these thoughts have nothing whatsoever to do with me, and they disperse. Doing this on a regular basis brings joy, a warmth and a knowledge that what we're doing is *good* for us - it's habit forming, and it's a good and beneficial habit to get into. Just as with my book shelves, I've come to love the empty spaces in my mind; whereas it was once crammed with controlling clutter from the past, it's now light and airy; thoughts creep in again, as they do, but then I take back control, repeat the process and reap the benefits.

On Faith

Faith is a personal thing that can't be conveyed - it burns within.

I'd just finished writing my chapter 'Observation' when a lady, with what she called a 'burning question' asked her friends online 'What keeps you faithful?' My reply was 'Faithful to what?' It was then I realised that up until that moment, I'd never thought about what faith is. Faith is a multi-faceted word that generally gets people's backs up, because of its strong religious connotations. I told a friend that I was writing a chapter about *faith* and before telling him anything about it I asked what his initial reaction was to the word. He replied 'My first thought on the word faith, is that all the miseries of the world have been ignored because of it.' Faith and religion are words so tightly entwined that they're practically indistinguishable; the meaning of both words can be confusing - too much pain and poisoned memories are associated with them. To consider 'faith' we first need to untangle it from religion - and any other interpretation or influence - so that it stands separate, untainted by dogma.

In my opinion, faith is often confused with belief and hope and all three are taken to mean the same thing - to me, that's an error. To believe, is not to *know* that something is true but rather it's a personal preference. We choose to believe something not because it's false or true but because it's convenient or suits our circumstances or culture to believe it - belief doesn't make something true. Hope, on the other hand, is waiting for a future event that may never arrive - rather like hoping that a bus we're waiting for will arrive, but not knowing for certain that it's coming. Faith is far harder to define and for this reason, hard to have. Faith is more like waiting for a bus, but knowing it *will* arrive at some point - there's no duality and therefore, no doubt. Faith is a combination of 'knowing' and 'trusting', without seeing, and with those comes a realisation that there's so much more we don't know about our world and can't know under our present circumstances. Faith is felt by our very essence and as our faith increases, it can't be shaken, as it isn't based on anything we've been taught. 'Hope' is a calculated risk, and 'belief' requires no evidence; both however, are roads that can lead to faith - it's embedded in our hearts. To try to explain the meaning of faith and how we can feel it is difficult because mere words just can't do it; we have to look *between* the lines where words don't exist.

Trying to describe faith, is rather like trying to describe what vanilla tastes like - we have to taste it for ourselves. Faith is something that grows and the process begins when we decide to look for truth - it grows alone, inside us. What keeps me faithful on my road and gives meaning to my life is knowing that in this physical world, there's absolutely nothing worth striving for. One way to think about this is to see what *changes* in the world, and through that process, realise what doesn't; we were once babies, grew taller, our features changed, our walk, the way we talk, what we know and what we don't know, but there's a part of us that doesn't change at all; it's been there since we were born - our awareness - and when we realise this our faith increases.

~~~

The uncovering of truth begins with the disposal of our illusions - by questioning. This is a materialistic world where commercialism thrives at the expense of human welfare. It's not always the *things* we create that do the damage, but that we create them without regard or thought for the good of our world or humanity. We don't see ourselves as *connected*; we're One, but have become separated, greedy and afraid. As long as we've desires and separation in the world or see life as one continuous effort, nothing will change. My faith began to develop when I saw there was nothing in this world that could make me complete - I'd reached an impasse. In other words, my faith grew when I let go of the struggle to become something or someone I wasn't. That left me rather in limbo; I didn't 'fit in' anywhere, but was still 'here' and knew I still had something to discover. It was when I stopped trying to fit in, that I realised I could *only* find completeness in myself; it's *only* when we're prepared to stop swimming upstream that the struggle ends.

In the past I'd sometimes go to a shopping centre or high street just to look around, but rarely found anything to buy because there was nothing I actually needed or wanted. Nothing could fill the space I felt between me and the rest of the world. I felt utterly bored and unchallenged in these vacuous environments. I found these shopping centres soulless, despite the presence of the heaving crowd and was amazed at the rush they were in to buy things, particularly at Christmas time. I'd sit in a café watching people coming and going, queuing to pay for things they probably didn't need, telling off their children (or not), while security guards strutted around keeping an eagle eye on 'potential' criminals. The noise, from the chatter of consumers, and each shop playing a different beat on its sound system was hypnotic and deafening. I could never concentrate on my reading or writing - things I loved to do in cafés. No matter where I went, I felt as though I was invisible - at times that was a lonely experience. Now I see this loneliness as having been my greatest *gift*; it enabled me to think long and hard about everything, and that's been paramount on my journey to find out who I am. Because of this feeling of being an *outsider* I was able to look at the world from a distance - from a different perspective. Among other things I saw clearly that even with their new purchases, the people wandering around were unhappy - there were no smiling faces - they were as lost in this world as I was. I didn't like what I saw and despite childhood longings, I no longer wanted to be a part of the crowd. What I needed to find out before anything else, was who I'm *not* and the above experiences helped me to do just that; the process of developing faith at this point, was one of negation.

We're driven by an innate desire to know or to discover 'something', and reminded of it *if* we choose to think about the inane rituals of our lives - we perform them but can't always see the emptiness they fill us with.

When I realised that everything we could want in this world was pointless I became down-hearted. However, this changed how I saw the world and I very soon lost all my fear of it; the root of fear must ultimately be a *fear of dying* and I pulled that root right out of the ground. Someone asked me recently what the last line of my autobiography would be and I said 'I came to this world with nothing and I'm leaving empty-handed.' I'd come to the realisation that there's a purpose to our lives but it's not to be found in the pursuit of meaningless activities or the accumulation of possessions that we can't take with us when we die. When we raise our consciousness levels there comes a time when possessions, gadgets and empty pursuits, although they have their place and can be great fun, lose their novelty appeal. What once served as a distraction from the knowledge that we have a higher purpose becomes empty and fatuous - it did for me at least.

Thinking about these things and the insanity of believing that the magnificent human body with all its non-physical accessories (thought, hope, love, laughter etc.), and the capability we have for carrying out atrocities has led me to know that there's far more to us than *composting* material and that this isn't apparent until we pay attention to it. Thinking about life and death and how little we do in between them is a valuable activity; we're born, educated, taught fear, work, retire and then die. There's a great deal more to us than we generally see and considering that last list, it's no wonder that in our suffering we occupy ourselves with trivial entertainments that simply pass the time, ignoring the inevitable finale.

The pieces fall into place when we eliminate regulatory, conditioned and limiting beliefs. In doing so, new levels of consciousness open up to us. However, when we continue to fill our lives with horror stories, how can we reasonably expect to find *peace* or *happiness* - all we're going to find are nightmares. Wherever we go we take ourselves with us; no matter how much we want to escape the drudgery of our lives, we can't do it without first freeing ourselves from our prisons. So for example, if we hear a new song that inspires us, as they do, we revel in the greatness of the artist or writer, but not in our own. We put our faith in others rather than in ourselves. Words in songs, films or books can invite us to become inspired, but they can't free us from ourselves no matter how many times we listen to them, unless that inspiration turns into action. In 'Just Around the Bend' I mentioned an experience I once had when a picture fell from my bedroom wall. Inexplicable events like these build faith, but only if we resist the urge to dismiss them as coincidence, or listen to the unconsidered explanations of others who think we've 'lost the plot'. As long as we don't use the voice we've been given, by allowing others to represent us, we'll remain in our shells of hope and belief.

Faith, in my opinion, is the assurance that I'm doing what's right for me - to write what I feel passionate about and to put my heart and soul into it. As long as we live with a need to fit in with things the world wants us to do we'll never find fulfillment. I know I'm best suited to writing from my heart and I've an enormous amount of faith in that. I fought it for many years and used to feel pretty inadequate when someone would say 'find what you love in the world and do it' and all I could think was 'I don't *love* anything'. But that was a lie and one of the reasons I couldn't write when I was younger was that I'd no faith in my ability, which meant no one else did either. In other words, I already knew what I loved but didn't feel competent enough to do it, or believe I could make a living at it. So I buried what was true for me and pursued some of the things society encourages us to pursue; romance, family, fitness, arts and crafts and being a 'good citizen', but I never found fulfillment in any of them. This attitude was further moulded by my father, who insisted that I find a profession that pays well - my father put income before anything else. However, I never found anything that made me feel at home in the world; something was still missing and when everyone was having a good time at parties and social venues, I was unable to enjoy them. I'd a huge void in my life that no-one nor anything could fill; still I continued the struggle to do things I deep down knew were not in my best interest. Once the ways of the world became pointless to me, I was free to find my own way, but as long as I tried to fit in somewhere I didn't belong, I was stuck. One change that occurs when faith develops is that this nagging feeling of not belonging ends; there's a deep and inexplicable knowing that we *do* belong. Accepting that I have a purpose, and that I'm not 'deluded' or 'need to see someone', has made my life meaningful and worthwhile. When we can't see the fruits of our efforts; they become as exhausting as running on the spot, and equally frustrating - we know that tomorrow will bring more of the same. We can be sure of the same depressive news in the newspapers, political arguments and sad faces worldwide. With faith comes a knowing that what we're pursuing *is* worthy of our attention; the faith we have is in *ourselves* and no longer in, or dependent on others.

Each one of us is unique and special - we have a talent we can fine tune; life is not pointless and doesn't have to be full of turmoil and pain. It's this way because we choose to enjoy the things that our system produces, even though we know full well the consequences of producing them. We demand more and more of the same because, to be frank, we don't know what else to do with our time. We unwisely choose to let others be responsible for the world we live in - we don't want, or know how to do it ourselves. We've put all our belief and hope in a system that destroys all things beautiful and all that has achieved is worldwide misery, guilt and shame. It can be difficult to understand why our world is the way it is, particularly at our level of consciousness, but we have to persevere with our journey, rather than give up. There's no point in waiting for the world to change - it isn't going to get any better. On the contrary, things are heading in the direction of more madness. We need to change the only thing we *can* change - ourselves - and have faith that everything else will work out just as it's meant to do. If we don't change, neither will our world. So whereas my friend's first thought was that 'all the miseries of the world had been ignored because of' *faith*, in fact, they've been ignored because of the lack of it.

Intention

Intention is a powerful energetic force
that creates our world.

What do I mean by intention? Intention is the outcome we want from any kind of action we take to achieve our purpose or goal, but it's not the action itself. Intention is what motivates us to do the things we do and if we're not motivated, we become lethargic, bored and mischievous. The intention behind our actions is not necessarily good; quite often we seek results that aren't good for us at all, like if we take revenge on someone, or act with menace in mind. For example, when we're driving along a motorway and feel a need to overtake the car in front, perhaps because the driver is too slow for our liking - perhaps he's driving an 'old banger' that we feel is less impressive than our own car. Our intention may be to show our ability to drive faster, to show off our car, or we may genuinely want to pass by without any mal-thoughts for the other driver. From my experiences in this situation, people mostly want to get 'in front' as though there were a stigma associated with driving behind another car, or to be more precise, another person; yes, I've done it too. I feel that one of the reasons we do these things is to try to prove to ourselves that we're in some way superior to the person in front of us; the ego loves to show off and it's also looking for security, or at least recognition. Most people who needlessly overtake tend to slow down once they're in front, which confirms that they just wanted to 'be there'. We're not generally honest with ourselves about our intentions; the excuses we make are the *permission* for our actions. In the example above, the driver may not like driving behind another car, but convinces himself that the car in front is driving too slowly, thereby justifying his own manoeuvres.

Another important part of our intentions is that they're not always clear, which is how we get into a bit of a muddle at times - often achieving something other than what we intended. When I didn't know what to do with my life the struggle was there because my intention wasn't clear; I didn't know what I really wanted, or so I kept telling myself. As a child I wanted a guitar, but I now know that it wasn't to become a brilliant guitarist - it was to write songs; I've always loved writing. Having unclear intentions is often a refusal to follow our heart, mostly because of a lack of faith in ourselves rather than in others. We push our dreams aside, not because of inability, but because if we set the intention we'd have to get on with it - we're expert procrastinators. It's for this reason that we become stuck in jobs that don't motivate us; we're doing them purely to pay the bills, buy new toys and prepare ourselves for retirement, rather than to fulfil our dreams - now not later. It's possible to love our work and when we love what we're doing, it isn't work at all. Okay, so maybe we can't make a good living doing what we really love to do, but as long as we can earn enough to live on, it's more fulfilling than the drudgery of working at something that doesn't inspire or challenge us. There's not much that's more depressing than spending our days doing things we don't like doing. When we get out of our own way, putting aside our fears and insecurities, it clears the path for us to achieve our full potential, though admittedly we can feel rather unsteady at first, it's a step in the right direction.

We don't always do the *right* things for the *right* reasons and not many of us consider the importance of our motives, before carrying out our actions. If we did, there are times that we'd be horrified by our own connivance, manipulative and often spiteful intentions. Take for example, Christmas time when we give gifts to family members, including those we give out of *obligation* to those we don't like, often buying a 'that'll do' present just to get it out of the way. We spend a lot of time choosing gifts for people we care for, but precious little on those we don't. I think we've all done that 'unwanted gift' thing from the previous year - we give it to someone else. I've known people deliberately buy someone a gift in the full knowledge that they wouldn't like it and others who like to 'balance' the scales, choosing gifts of equal value to the ones they expect to receive - this is not the same as a prior arrangement to spend a fixed amount on each other. Either way, this type of gift giving is more perfunctory than a well-intentioned thought out gift. There's another way we like to give gifts and that's in order to gain the approval or love of others - this intention never gets the desired results and that's because money can't buy love or approval - nothing can.

I 'over-gave' gifts for many years for the wrong reasons - to gain approval. All I gained were people around me who were no good for me. I attracted people who waited around in my life for the next gift, or others who took offence at them. One of my sisters took offence. If she came to my house and admired something I had, I'd give it to her, but she took this to be an act of superiority on my part rather than a loving and generous one. In the end, she stopped admiring anything and I refrained from giving her things. We know why we give things to people, but can't know the mind or trigger that we pull when we give a gift to someone else. Although I gave things for what I considered to be the right reasons - I was never materialistic - there was an underlying intention on my part to gain their approval. From my sister's point of view, she thought I was suggesting that she couldn't afford to buy these things on her own.

We're One; we really are. If we take time to reflect on this, we see it's not just our intentions that count, but the collective intention of everyone else as well. Intention is energy and when the energy we put out isn't good, neither is what comes back. In the case of our intentionally giving someone a gift they won't want, along with the *gift* we're giving negative energy and this comes back to us, usually in the form of a lack of gratitude from a disappointed and underwhelmed recipient, and maybe a gift *we* don't like in the future - repercussions and revenge ensuring the continuity of the cycle. Multiply that by everyone who gives just for the sake of it and that's a lot of negative energy bouncing around. If you don't believe all this, observe how the feel-good level of the lights on the trees, the tinsel and the carols at Christmas time is lowered by the chaos and frenetic activity of shoppers. Also, observe yourself when you're giving gifts or receiving them - be aware of your heartfelt intentions, and disappointments. How would you feel if you gave a gift to someone who didn't give one back to you? We've lost the art of *giving* and not expecting anything in return.

I remember once being in a hurry to cross a road that wasn't very busy, and didn't feel like walking the distance to the zebra crossing. So I crossed where I was, because I consider myself to be intelligent enough to know when it's safe to do so. The only vehicle that passed me was a lone motorcyclist and though I wasn't in his way at all, he tooted his horn, shook his fist at me and yelled that there was a pedestrian crossing further along the road. His intention here was not for my well-being, but to throw *rules* at me that he valued a bit too highly, for not obeying them in the same way as he would, or *wouldn't* as the case may be. When we tell others how to behave correctly, too often we don't live by our own convictions; listening to what others say and how they say it is a good guide to knowing their intentions. When we act in the way the motorcyclist did, our motives are wrong and therefore, our intentions aren't in line with our best interest; our intention is to complain about something someone else is doing. People like the motorcyclist go out of their way to criticise, but don't take the time to look at themselves - the only true way to learn about *our*selves. Ironically, the man was more interested in telling me off for what I was doing, rather than what he was doing;

riding a motorbike, yelling angrily and shaking his fist at me. Too often our intention is to get other people to behave in the way *we* think they should, rather than considering how *we* behave.

When we analyse these things we begin to think about our intentions, but only if we don't get too caught up in the analysis itself. When we do this we no longer have to ask for the opinions or approval of others - intention alone will get us what we want. The problem here is that we don't always *know* what we want and this is why so many people are unhappy. When I decided to finally write this book, my intention was that the book would be found by and help anyone that was ready to hear what I'd written on its pages - it was also to remove the block that told me I couldn't do it. Despite the initial *discouragement* from some people, my intention was already set and therefore, productive. I didn't need approval or want advice and because my intention was set, didn't need any motivation either. Writing became my life, day and night, as with this book; I'm doing what I love to do the most and trusting that the universe will guide me. When our intention is set, it will bear fruit - what kind of fruit depends on whether our intention is good or bad.

The most important aspect of our intentions is that as far as possible we have to live in a way that's in line with them, rather than in opposition. If we intend to become an author for example, we have to get on with the writing - the book won't write itself. After deciding that we've a skill in writing it's important to know what we want to write about and in what genre. It doesn't matter if it isn't popular or even liked; if we feel a need to express ourselves in a particular way then we must never be put off by anyone else's negativity. Most people offer discouragement rather than encouragement - follow your own heart and don't listen to them. If we spend all our spare time watching television or socialising rather than getting down to the business of writing, then we're not living in line with our intentions and shouldn't be surprised or disappointed that no book is produced. Gaining confidence and tuning into our talents requires a lot of sacrifice, particularly in our spare time. We all have a talent that we can hone - at least one - and deep down we know what it is. Only fear prevents us from living in a way that's in our best interest - passionately. A life without passion is never rewarding but a life with passion gets us up in the mornings full of motivation for the day ahead; however, waiting for our purpose or passion to come knocking on our door is both pointless and disappointing - we *have* to find them for ourselves. The next important thing to do with our talent or passion is to complete whatever it is we intend to do.

Intention, will bring our dreams to life if we dare to start the ball rolling, as it were - too often we lie to ourselves about our true intentions. It's easy to become distracted or disillusioned along the way by the negativity of others, because we're in the habit of not taking chances - even if we're bored stiff. We like to stay with what we believe to be *secure* and don't tend to need much discouragement. The biggest discouragements, as always, come from our own mind, particularly with regard to things like fitness, diet or any attempt to change from our familiar way of life.

When we examine intention itself, it becomes clear what our intentions really are, and the phrase 'the road to hell is paved with good intentions', begins to make sense. Suppose we consider taking up a sport because we want, or have been encouraged by our doctor for example, to get 'fit'. We might put it off because we 'can't afford' the right kit. They aren't necessary for our project, but we convince ourselves that they are and so put off starting whatever it is we claim we want to do. If we do buy the 'kit', it all too often gets left in the cupboard after one or two seasonal attempts to learn our chosen sport and it's never used again. Often we can repeat this procedure of buying different kits as we try out and test other sports or hobbies in an attempt to find something we *can* excel in. On a similar vein, how many kitchens contain 'must have' good intentioned gadgets consigned to the back of cupboards - juicers for example; we don't know what we want and therefore, can't set our intention - our initial enthusiasm soon dwindles.

Changing our habits can be difficult, particularly when our intention isn't set to do so; for example, when attempting to stop smoking, or any other habit; we *claim* we want to give them up, and that we *will*, but we don't mean it - our 'intention' sits firmly at the starting block, and we remain forever in a state of 'trying', but never achieving. To get an intention off the starting block takes commitment, if we're ever to realise our goal - we have to keep at it until it's achieved. This is a difficult concept to grasp in our 'instant gratification' society. A student doesn't become a master overnight - it takes effort; we can't become an instant lawyer, scientist or artist - there's no 'just add water' to achievement.

Humanity is One

We're the only obstacle we need to overcome.

We're humanity; we're complex, wonderfully made and capable of amazing feats - our creativity knows no bounds. Sadly, this creativity is used to destroy and separate, rather than to unite us. We create things of great beauty, but then ascribe to them a value leading to a need to protect them behind iron bars, security cameras, guards and electric fences. We give things of 'value' more admiration, protection and care than we do the people who created them. It can be alarming to see people pushing and shoving fellow human beings out of the way, in their rush to acquire these *possessions* - some of us are even prepared to kill for them.

There's so much we've forgotten about that's common to every human being. We want to live in a peaceful world, where we can live without fear and come and go as we please. However, our history is at best 'disturbing' and prevents this sort of freedom. We live so close together, but we can never *really* know each other - we don't allow anyone near to that part of us we guard so closely. Unable to show vulnerability, because we fear it would leave us prey to those who'd perceive it as weakness, we're reluctant to take that first step to freedom - no one wants to go first. Because of this division we're on the offensive like a coiled snake ready to strike anyone who encroaches our space. At the heart of this posturing there's a sense of loss and confusion about our origin and destination. This hostility is manifested as an 'it's none of your business' attitude, which means we don't like anyone prying past the personal wall that we call *private* - we're walking 'Keep Out' signs. The confusion causes us so much pain that we bury the emotions deeply in order to function in our world, where we're encouraged to be attractive, mindless, afraid and tough - paradoxically to be their opposites as well. We're also encouraged to fend for ourselves and compete with each other for 'status', larger homes and faster cars. Because we're encouraged to behave in so many conflicting ways by people we don't know, it's hardly surprising we don't have a clue who we are.

We live in a world where we don't appreciate each other, neither do we feel appreciated, loved or wanted. A world in which there's so much hatred that we kill, injure or hurt each other with no good reason, leaving others homeless and starving; it's mankind who's responsible for this situation, and mankind that remains silent. Until we see this, it will remain difficult for us to change this world into a better place to live in. Some of you may argue that there are those who *are* loved; I'd have to disagree with you, as I'm talking about a love that isn't conditional or ephemeral. I'm also speaking about the majority and not the few who realise that this love is true. A love that we miss and long to return to - a love that has no need of money, masks or possessions, isn't selective or conditional and is literally, priceless. We don't have faith or see that a love like this exists because we're too focused on our separation; nations, countries, towns, families, cultures - just some of the causes of the many problems of our world. These levels of separation are increasing as parents become separated from their children, teachers from their pupils and employers from their employees; of course vice versa too. The concept of our separation and what we may have become separated from are things worth thinking about - essential if we want to close the gap between us.

Humanity is losing its ability to communicate with itself having become dependent on the mass media, and a plethora of electronic devices. We've one language for parents and another for children - thus separating them. For these reasons we're selfish and alert only to the ways we can survive, along with those closest to us. Close or not we generally get into arguments and debates, where no one person gives way to another - each tries to push their own agenda forward. Humanity looks outward for solutions to the problems it doesn't fully admit to, and we search for 'home sweet homes' that we can't hold onto forever, no matter how much we want, insure, decorate or tweak them. These homes become somewhere we *claim* as our very own and from that we get a sense of *belonging* to both the property and our families. However, I'd suggest that homes built for our security are actually prisons; outside them we don't feel safe and inside, we lock ourselves securely in - we think. Instead of being One humanity, we've become *one* nation or some other group; *one*, behind a barrier which is constructed upon the conditions laid down by others. We're physically one, rather than spiritually and the result of this is that we're suspicious of each other to the point of exclusion and prior judgement, even of those we've never met. By contrast, we allow those we don't trust to take charge of the society we created - we're quite mad!

~~~

We repeat the same activities day after day and apart from a few variations, depending on whether it's the weekend or we're on holiday, not much changes. A quick calculation reveals that I've brushed my teeth approximately 40,000 times in my lifetime and that's just one of the many daily repetitive rituals we perform. This is why we like things to celebrate such as birthdays, Christmas or some sporting event and mark these dates on a calendar, erasing each day that leads up to them with an 'X' - rather than living it, we *kiss* our lives goodbye. It's a paradox; we're excited about *waiting* for future events, yet frustrated by having to wait for them;

we want to be *there* rather than *here*. We wouldn't want to celebrate going to work, shopping, a new television program or the onset of war, but these are a real part of our daily lives. No wonder we get excited about the latest gadgets - they break monotony, give us something to hope for *and* something to play with. That we never celebrate the monotonous nature of our lives has got to be worth thinking about, considering most of us suffer with the incessant boredom of them; why else do we look forward to future events. Life itself should be a celebration. The sister of a friend of mine was asked what she'd do if she knew she was going to die in her sleep; her reply was 'I'd go to bed early'. That's how low the spirit of humanity is right now. Something's very wrong when we celebrate things that don't matter or understand the true meanings of, ignoring the things that do - like life and each other.

As mentioned earlier, we've so much in common, including wonderful bodies that are perfectly suited to perform so many varied tasks. We just have to recognise our conditioning and then unlock our magnificent potential - we all have it. We create the most intricate devices: such as, the clockwork components for a watch, we can study the stars, dance on ice, sing in choirs, imagine unknown life forms and think about how we came into being. We compose beautiful music, write poetry and paint masterpieces that transport us to other worlds and / or invoke tears and emotions, inspiring generations to come - we can do so much good. Thinking is a wonderful ability - everyone is able to do it. Sadly, due to the pressures of life, we're chasing our tails and consequently our abilities are seldom realised. We marvel at people on talent shows who are discovered quite by chance, but rarely get the opportunity to find out what we're capable of ourselves. When we do find our talent, it's often shelved until we've more time or we retire - if we've got enough energy left. One of the things we've all got in common is our uniqueness; we're all special in our own way.

Generally, people don't question how we came to have so many abilities. There are those who believe the human being is merely a universal 'accident' of evolution; in my opinion, this view is utter nonsense. Today, we're focused on the physical and our desires, but tend to ignore our vastly superior metaphysical qualities. People who think otherwise haven't given the matter any serious thought - our exceptional qualities are crystal clear. Have you ever taken the time to wonder about how we see, touch, taste, smell or hear anything? How many other creatures can claim to be so brilliant or versatile?

It's about time humanity realised how magnificent it really is and stopped behaving as though each one of us doesn't matter. Life doesn't have to be full of monotony or fear; it's this way because we agree to it, and choose to be afraid, rather than say 'No' to the things that aren't good for us. The world has many problems and many unhappy people living in it, but we don't have to be that way too. No matter how miserable we feel we ought to become, or how guilty we feel about being content whilst others are suffering, we won't make the world into a better place to live in. We make the world happier by being happier in it - every move counts and the more people that make them, the better. This is what 'free will' - for want of a better term - is really all about; we can stay in the gloom and unhappy crowd or leave and *reconnect* to our point of Origin. We're infinite beings; we can choose to persevere with our pain and suffering or leave the field. There are those who claim that not keeping up with the disastrous affairs of our planet means that we don't care, but I'll say to them what good does playing 'oh no ... how awful' do for the suffering of others? It never *has* done any good and it never will or it would have done so by now. Only coming together again will help the suffering of others and to do this we need to look at the world objectively, rather than in the subjective and selfish way that's become a habit. People are suffering, not because they were born in the wrong country, but because suffering is being inflicted on them.

We can raise our consciousness level, but first we have to be prepared to find out why it's so low. It's no good just dabbling with 'cotton wool' philosophy, or sticking 'I love me' notes all over the place - they only work temporarily, if at all, because we're not looking at the root causes of our state of mind. If anything, when we read these notes we reinforce self-hatred because we're lying and we know it. As we read them the stronger feeling is *I don't love myself at all*. For me, it's nothing more than spraying an air freshener into a stale room - it soon smells stale again. When we question the way we've come to know this world and realise that like a stagnant pond it won't change without our intervention, we can begin to put things right. Until the dirty water is cleaned of the 'litter of ages', we'll remain exactly as we are - wallowing in our own filth, blaming each other for our condition. We can't change Jenny Jones next door, but we can change how we think about her and see that she suffers just like everyone else. We all have different mechanisms to cope with living in this world and that can be expressed as aggression, illness, self-deprecation, depression, judgement of others and much more. However, the root of the problem is the same - our separation.

~~~

How is it possible to see ourselves as One again? By widening our perspective. When we pay attention to our world it becomes apparent that despite each one of us having a unique character and point of view, we share a great deal more in common. By recognising this, we bring together again parts that have been separated for far too long. After all:

- We want to be heard.
- We've been hurt.
- We're unaware of what other people are feeling.
- We've a talent.
- We share this home.
- We're searching for love.
- We want recognition.
- We're afraid.
- We want an easier life.
- We're imperfect.
- We *must* die.
- We're killing time and don't know why.

I could easily fill up two pages with this list. There's so much more that we share but we've forgotten this because of our separation from each other. Regarding the last point I made, the reason we don't know why we're killing time is that we don't take time to consider these things - we're very good at procrastinating. When we pay attention to our similarities, rather than our differences, we reconnect to the whole. When we connect to the whole and realise that we're a part of it, selfishness becomes a thing of the past - it's our selfish and pompous acts that bring about and enforce our separation. When we criticise someone else, because they're different, we alienate ourselves from them. It's not so difficult to focus on what we have in common and it's much more satisfying than focusing on what we don't. When we do this our intention, rather than being competitive, judgemental or derogatory, is noble.

On a practical level, when those nasty old thoughts peep through the cracks, we can watch them closely. So for example, we see coming towards us an unkempt person wearing old worn clothing. We can look at them in one of two ways - with a critical or compassionate eye. Mostly our first thoughts are critical - that's our conditioning and it's deep-seated. We can take charge of our thoughts and recognise that this is a person just like us - perhaps less fortunate. They may be suffering in ways we can't comprehend; we can't see the world through their eyes and we can't be aware of the cause of their pain or suffering - it's possible they're entirely alone in this world. By challenging our original critical thought and replacing it with a non-judgemental one, we then see the person in a totally different light. If we take it several steps further it becomes clear that their predicament isn't their own fault, but one brought about by the society we created, and sustain. As well as considering why a person may be wearing worn out clothing, it would be an interesting exercise to ask ourselves why we're so bothered by it; what is it about us that needs to criticise others and in what way are we more 'deserving' than they are? If we persevere in this way, then the space that separates us becomes smaller and we begin to look at others compassionately, rather than critically. When we keep catching those thoughts it becomes apparent that we're not so different; we're One. By the same token, paying close attention to the unrelenting thoughts that turn in our heads when we're trying to get to sleep, we'll find that these will change too. However, if we're determined to think that we're better than others all we do is *increase* the space that separates us - isolating ourselves - psychologically and physically, from the rest of humanity.

In this chapter, I've attempted to explain my thoughts on how we're all One. Putting into words this abstract concept is not an easy task. However, once we grasp the concept, our separation from each other becomes obvious, and if we embrace it, our lives take on a more meaningful direction - life is no longer pointless or passé; we realise that we're not and never have been alone - we cease the struggle to become something we're not. Have you ever seen a shoal of fish swimming together or a flock of starlings in flight? They move as one, for the common good, and none of them fight with each other for space or first place, yet each one plays their part in the dance. If you haven't seen these you can find videos online -watching them is worth the effort. Whenever we gather together *en masse* we're all powerful and intentional, just like the fish and starlings, but as individuals our power and beauty are greatly reduced. When we've One mind, we can achieve so many marvellous things in this world. Sadly, we use this collective power for the wrong things, particularly war. Imagine a world where we gather together for the good of the planet and mankind; a world where we allow each other to develop our innate talents; a world without threat, fear, borders or corruption. I don't know about you but I for one would love to experience it. We're humanity and no matter how individual or superior we think we are, we're part of a greater whole. We all belong together and we always will. When we hurt each other what we're really doing is hurting ourselves - damaging the world in which we must all continue to live.

We're One

We fear the darkness, yet choose to reside within it.

One day soon we'll re-gather

And wonder from where this madness stemmed

And how we thought we'd never mend

The gaping space that spanned between

Our unadulterated love for each other

And turned it into war and corruption

As we ran riot

Destroying not only ourselves, but others

With our faces devoid of empathy.

You,

My neighbour who I've loved forever

Looked at me with hatred in your eyes

Because you didn't recognise me and

Because I recognised you and said

'Bonjour' with a smile

That you could not return.

You,

My neighbour who obeys without question

Those who do not bless you

Or value your divinity because

They prefer that you live in fear of

The power you once gave them.

You,

My neighbour who has forgotten

On what sacred ground your feet walk upon

And the humble people you trample

Beneath your vanity and pride

Without ever knowing they're there.

One day soon we'll re-gather

And know from where this madness grows

And know we always knew we'd close

The gaping space that spanned between

Our unadulterated love for each other.

Who am I?

Just around the bend the music is still playing, but it's at a higher frequency.

I've reached the end of my second section, and so much has changed for me. Let me correct that statement - *I've* changed so much in me. Obviously, you're still here in my pages, and I'd like to thank you for your company, and for sharing my journey - it has been a life-changing experience for me, and I hope it has for you too. When I see a photograph of myself, I don't recognise it as me. When I see my earlier writings, I don't recognise that I wrote them - the words seem to have never left my fingers. The past doesn't exist for me and it doesn't exist for you either - changing our perspective makes this perfectly clear. When we realise that neither the past nor future exist it's inevitable that, even if only in small glimpses, we begin, with increasing frequency, to experience the Now. Everything is connected, here and Now. I'm entirely responsible for my life; I never once imagined I'd ever say a thing like that.

It's all me

Everywhere I go

Left and up

Down and right

Turning myself inside out

And back to front

And in so many other directions

That I have no words for, because -

I

Am the mother of my child

I

Gave birth to it

I

Fed and nurtured it

I

Made my child

What she is today

And created her each and every way

She became an obsession

An un-treasured possession

That I valued, not, in any graceful way

Abandoned and rejected -

She'd

Been left to decay

Then

I

Rose

From her ashes

Dazed and confused

Deconstructed the parts

I'd cruelly abused

I reached and climbed

Every hill I could find

Then in Awe I relished

The Silence of my mind

No-thing at all

Had obviously changed

But

Somehow

Something

Had been rearranged.

NOTES

NOTES

NOTES

About the Author

Renée Paule was born in London and was brought up in an orphanage, despite having two living parents. Subjected to mental and physical cruelty, the trauma she suffered left her with twelve years of almost total amnesia. Six marriages later (four official), she chose to 'take stock' and began a process of questioning everything in her world.

Her take on life changed dramatically following a profound experience revealing the connection between herself and the Universe - there's no separation. With this realisation, she no longer accepted the 'face-value' world she'd once thought of as the norm.

Renée Paule wishes to share this knowledge and show how a change of perspective can provide an alternative to the topsy-turvy world that Humanity, on the whole, accepts as an inevitable way of life.

She now lives in Ireland.

www.reneepaule.com

46366770R00096

Printed in Poland
by Amazon Fulfillment
Poland Sp. z o.o., Wrocław